Dying to Self

Finding Life in Christ

Amy Hernandez

Developed as a study course by Emmaus Correspondence School, founded in 1942.

Dying to Self
Amy Hernandez

Published by:
Emmaus Worldwide
PO Box 1028
Dubuque, IA 52004-1028
phone: (563) 585-2070
email: info@emmausworldwide.org
website: EmmausWorldwide.org

First Edition 2019 (AK '19)
Reprinted 2020 (AK '19)

ISBN 978-1-59387-477-3

Code: DTS

Adapted from previous work titled "Unstuck" published in 2015 by ECS ministries.

Printed in the United States of America

Course Overview

There is a war raging within yourself. It is the battle against the flesh, the "old you" which is completely opposed to the Spirit's work in your life. In the book of Galatians, Paul teaches us that we are to crucify the flesh and walk by the Spirit. This course will help you expose your flesh, provides four Biblical methods of dying to self, and explores the areas of your life in which you must walk by the Spirit's power.

The good news is that when you die to self and walk in the Spirit, you will find life and freedom in Christ.

Lessons You Will Study

Student Instructions

This Emmaus course is designed to help you know God through a better understanding of the Bible and know how it applies to your life. However, this course can never take the place of the Bible itself. The Bible is inexhaustible, and no course could give the full meaning of its truth. If studying this course is the end goal, it will become an obstacle to your growth; if it is used to inspire and equip you for your own personal study of the Bible, then it will achieve its goal. As you study the Bible using this course, prayerfully ask God to reveal His truth to you in a powerful way.

Course Sections

This course has three parts: the *lessons*, the *exams* and the *exam sheet*.

The Lessons

Each lesson is written to help explain truths from the Bible. Read each lesson through at least twice—once to get a general idea of its content, then again, slowly, looking up any Bible references given. You should always have your Bible opened to the verses or passage being studied. It is important that you read the Bible passages referenced, as some questions in the exams may be based on the Bible text.

To look up a Bible verse, keep in mind passages in the Bible are listed by book, chapter, and verse. For instance, 2 Peter 1:21 refers to the second book of Peter, chapter 1, and verse 21. At the beginning of every Bible, there is a table of contents which lists the names of the books of the Bible and tells the page number on which each book begins. For practice, look up 2 Peter in the table of contents and turn to the page number listed; then find the chapter and verse.

The Exams

At the end of each lesson, there is an exam to assess your knowledge of the course material and the Bible passages. The exams contain multiple choice and/or True/False (T/F) questions. After you have studied a lesson, complete the exam for that lesson by recording your answers on the exam sheet that has been provided. If you have difficulty answering the questions, re-read the lesson or use the Bible as a reference.

Please note, it is best not to answer the questions based on what you *think* or have *always believed*. The questions are designed to find out if you understand the material in the course and the Bible.

What Do You Say?

In addition to the multiple choice section, each exam also contains a *What Do You Say?* question. These questions are designed for your personal reflection and to help you express your ideas and feelings as you process the lesson's content.

The Exam Sheet

Use the exam sheet provided by your group leader or instructor. When you have determined the right answer to a question on an exam, fill in the corresponding letter on the exam sheet. If you do not have someone who could provide an exam sheet, you can download one at www.emmausworldwide.org/pages/exam-sheets

Submitting the Exam Sheet

When you have answered all the exam questions on the exam sheet, check them carefully. Fill in your contact information and submit your completed exam sheet to your group leader or instructor or the organization from which you received it (several options for submission are shown at next page).

OPTION 1: Send to your group leader or instructor

If you know your group leader or instructor, give them your completed exam sheet or mail it to the address listed here (if blank, go to option 2).

OPTION 2: Send to Emmaus Worldwide's head office

If no address is listed above, or if you do not know if you have a group leader or instructor and are unsure of where to send your exam sheet, choose one of the following:

MAIL the exam sheet to

Emmaus Worldwide
PO Box 1028
Dubuque, IA 52004-1028

OR

EMAIL a scan or photo

of both sides of the exam sheet to this email address:

Exams@EmmauWorldwide.org

Receiving Your Results

You will receive back your graded exam sheet (through the same method it was submitted, either mail or email), including your final grade and a personal response from your group leader or instructor or Emmaus Worldwide.

Introduction

Opposition is exhausting. We instinctively avoid it, but in the spiritual life, opposition can be a good thing. In his letter to the Galatians, Paul tells us that the desires of the flesh and the desires of the Spirit are in opposition. The Spirit and the flesh constantly oppose or work against each other. If the Spirit is gaining control, the flesh will resist; if the flesh is insisting on fulfilling its desires, the Spirit will tug against the natural self-satisfaction of your flesh. Either way, the struggle is healthy. It is better than giving in or giving up. Paul says, "If we live by the Spirit, let us also walk by the Spirit" (Gal. 5:25).

The Spirit and the flesh constantly oppose or work against each other.

How does this work? Do you walk by the Spirit first and thus achieve death of the flesh? Or do you put the flesh to death and thus achieve walking by the Spirit? How can you know if you are walking by the Spirit or if you are putting confidence in your flesh? Can you be certain that your efforts in the Christian life are completely powered by the Spirit? This course will help you expose what opposes the Spirit—the flesh—and the many ways it is lurking about. This is all for one goal: to crucify it.

The lessons of this course are divided into three sections:

Prepare the Flesh for Death

The first step is tackling the opposition—the flesh. Because Satan can pinpoint the tendencies of your flesh with sharp accuracy, you need to be aware of them as well. You must know where your flesh is most vulnerable. You must know your flesh's weaknesses better than your enemy does.

- *Lesson 1:* The Flesh
- *Lesson 2:* Identifying Our Flesh
- *Lesson 3:* Dying to Self

Die to Self Daily

Once identified, your flesh must be crucified. That's where you take up your cross every day. We will examine in Scripture four tools or methods that God uses to help us put the flesh to death. We will also explore how the flesh distorts the God-given purpose of those tools.

- *Lesson 4:* Weakness
- *Lesson 5:* Suffering
- *Lesson 6:* Humility
- *Lesson 7:* Repentance

Walk Empowered by the Spirit

Finally, by examining the role of the Holy Spirit in our lives, we will learn why we must walk in complete dependence on the Spirit for truth, love, and prayer. We will also learn to recognize signs that the flesh is working hard to trap us and keep us stuck.

- *Lesson 8:* Walking in Truth, Part 1
- *Lesson 9:* Walking in Truth, Part 2
- *Lesson 10:* Walking in Love
- *Lesson 11:* Walking in Prayer
- *Lesson 12:* Finding Life in Christ

Jesus said, "… If anyone would come after me, let him deny himself and take up his cross and follow me" (Matt. 16:24). My prayer is that you will want to follow Christ by taking up your cross daily, by living every day with a death sentence.

Dying to self is the key to becoming free to walk by the Spirit.

LESSON 1

The Flesh

The light has come into the world, and people loved the darkness rather than the light because their works were evil. For everyone who does wicked things hates the light and does not come to the light, lest his works should be exposed. (John 3:19-20)

We have a natural inclination in us to sin; it is called "the flesh" or "the natural man." We are born with this tendency to put ourselves first, to satisfy our needs, to be selfish. Our sin stains us, bringing spiritual death. The only cure for our sin is the blood of Jesus Christ. And yet we, who have put our faith in Jesus and are spiritually reborn, continue to struggle with sin, confused by the weakness that allows sin and defeat in our lives. How can this be? Why is it so hard to be victorious over sin?

It is because there is something fighting against the Spirit's work in our lives. Something that will do everything in its power to bring us down. It is the *flesh* that remains in us—that "old self" which continually seeks to drag us back into sin. It *wants* us to live in darkness. It is incredibly devious and crafty.

The flesh seeks to drag us back into sin. It *wants* us to live in darkness.

If we are not aware of the flesh, the way it works, and how to overcome it by the power of the Spirit, we will continue to walk in defeat. So let's begin by looking at some of the ways in which the flesh works.

The Flesh Desires

Consider Eve, who lived in the most beautiful place ever encountered on earth. She got her fruit right off the tree when it was ripe, full of delicious flavor. She could satisfy her hunger anytime with a divine banquet of food. And if that wasn't enough, she had intimate evening walks with God Himself. The best of everything was hers! What more could she want?

God had told Adam and Eve that they were free to eat from any tree in the garden except for one. If they did eat of that one tree, they would die (Gen. 2:16-17). Adam and Eve took this so seriously that they wouldn't even touch the fruit on that tree (Gen. 3:3). You'd think that Eve would be content enough to leave it alone. You'd think Satan would not have had a chance of deceiving her when all her needs were already satisfied. So what in the world made Eve want to eat the fruit? Certainly not need. What was deadly suddenly became desirable.

> When the woman saw that the tree was good for food, and that it was a delight to the eyes, and that the tree was desirable to make one wise, she took from its fruit and ate; and she gave also to her husband with her, and he ate. (Gen. 3:6)

Why did Eve have a strong desire to taste what would bring death? What had changed?

The change was in how Eve saw the fruit. It looked *good* and *delightful* and *desirable.* She saw what she couldn't have. Desire was triggered and she longed to satisfy that desire with what was bad for her.

Scripture says:

> For from within, out of the heart of men, proceed the evil thoughts, fornications, thefts, murders, adulteries, deeds of coveting, and wickedness, as well as deceit, sensuality, envy, slander, pride, and foolishness. All these evil things proceed from within and defile the man. (Mark 7:21-23)

> You lay aside the old self, which is being corrupted in accordance with the lusts of deceit. (Eph. 4:22)

> The heart is more deceitful than all else and is desperately sick; Who can understand it? I, the Lord, search the heart, I test the mind. (Jer. 17:9-10a)

> But encourage one another day after day, as long as it is still called "Today," so that none of you will be hardened by the deceitfulness of sin. (Heb. 3:13)

Like Eve, you are susceptible to being deceived by your flesh. I don't mean that the flesh is playing an innocent little trick on you. I'm saying that the flesh deceives you with *deadly desire.*

The Flesh Appeals

Adam sees Eve holding the forbidden fruit towards him, inviting him to eat with her. Has he thought through the implications of what she has done? She's eaten the fruit and death will separate them. Now he has a choice. He can choose to not eat the fruit and have eternity with God, separated from Eve, or he can take the fruit, eat it, and be restored to Eve, but separated from God. He chooses separation from God. I wonder what was more appealing to Adam: the fruit or Eve.

Let's look at another Biblical example—Achin. When the Lord broke down the walls of Jericho before the people of Israel, God commanded the people not to take anything from the city. But a man named Achin did. He later explained,

> When I saw among the spoil a beautiful cloak from Shinar, and 200 shekels of silver, and a bar of gold weighing 50 shekels, then I coveted them and took them. (Josh. 7:21, ESV)

His eye spotted that beautiful cloak and he was hooked. He gave in to the cravings of his flesh. His lust eventually led to a disastrous defeat for the whole nation.

The Flesh Enslaves

In the flesh, we trust ourselves to know what is good for us; we believe our desires will bring us freedom and doubt the goodness of God's desires for us. Don't be deceived—the flesh does not desire our good. It desires *slavery*.

The Israelites' life in Egypt had been slavery. Then God miraculously led an entire nation of 2 million people out of slavery in one of the most powerful kingdoms of the time. But when they got trapped between the Red Sea and Pharaoh's army, they said,

> Is it because there were no graves in Egypt that you have taken us away to die in the wilderness? Why have you dealt with us in this way, bringing us out of Egypt? Is this not the word that we spoke to you in Egypt, saying, "leave us alone that we may serve the Egyptians"? For it would have been better for us to serve the Egyptians than to die in the wilderness. (Ex. 14:11-12)

They preferred slavery over death.

God revealed His incredible power to save them by leading them between two walls of water and then drowning Pharaoh's army in that same water. But after a month of living in the desert, they said,

> Would that we had died by the Lord's hand in the land of Egypt, when we sat by the pots of meat, when we ate bread to the full; for you have brought us out into this wilderness to kill this whole assembly with hunger. (Ex. 16:3)

They would rather be slaves with pots of meat than live with their God in the wilderness.

At Rephidim, there was no water, and the people said,

> Why, now, have you brought us up from Egypt, to kill us and our children and our livestock with thirst? (Ex. 17:3)

They would rather be slaves in Egypt than be thirsty and free.

> We remember the fish which we used to eat free in Egypt, the cucumbers and the melons and the leeks and the onions and the garlic, but now our appetite is gone. There is nothing at all to look at except this manna. (Num. 11:5-6)

> Why then have you [Moses] brought the Lord's assembly into this wilderness, for us and our beasts to die here? Why have you made us come up from Egypt, to bring us in to this wretched place? It is not a place of grain or figs or vines or pomegranates, nor is there water to drink. (Num. 20:4-5)

Like the Israelites, our flesh hates to suffer and will always choose to please itself, even if that means being enslaved.

Flesh desires *slavery*.

Moses had a different attitude.

> By faith Moses, when he had grown up, refused to be called the son of Pharaoh's daughter; choosing rather to endure ill-treatment with the people of God, than to enjoy the passing pleasures of sin; considering the reproach of Christ greater riches than the treasures of Egypt; for he was looking to the reward. (Heb. 11:24-26)

The flesh wants you to go back to "Egypt," back to slavery in sin, but that isn't who you are in Christ.

> Therefore there is now no condemnation for those who are in Christ Jesus. For the law of the Spirit of life in Christ Jesus has set you free from the law of sin and of death. For what the Law could not do, weak as it was through the flesh, God did: sending His own Son in the likeness of sinful flesh and as an offering for sin, He condemned sin in the flesh, so that the requirement of the Law might be fulfilled in us, who do not walk according to the flesh, but according to the Spirit. (Rom. 8:1-4)

The flesh enslaves us to sin, to the fulfillment of selfish desires. The flesh compels us to look inward to satisfy our needs, but the flesh is never satisfied.

The Flesh Deceives

I have heard that when a pilot flies through a storm, his senses can tell him something totally different from what the instrument panel says. He has to fight against what his senses tell him to do and follow something else. His senses are untrustworthy.

Feelings can often act as voices of the flesh that give terrible directions. Follow them and, more often than not, you'll find yourself circling deeper into the storm. Argue and reason with them and you'll do no better.

The flesh will deceive and mislead you; it will never guide you into the truth. The Spirit is your only guide to the truth.

Imagine playing tennis by yourself. If you keep returning the ball, the game will never stop. Engaging with the flesh is like that. The flesh will throw things at you that will draw your attention away from the Spirit's directions. If you want the Spirit to guide you, you have to stop hitting the flesh's ball back. Don't agree when the flesh tells you that you are right to justify yourself. Don't get distracted by how much you've been hurt. Don't play the game with the flesh by affirming your feelings. Don't throw up your hands and say that prayer doesn't work. And definitely don't try to find your way out by reasoning your way out.

The flesh desires, appeals, enslaves, and deceives. This is your opposition. Expose it!

LESSON 1 EXAM

Use the exam sheet at the back of the course to complete your exam.

1. **According to Jeremiah 17:9, what is the most deceitful part of us?**
   A. The brain
   B. The heart
   C. The mouth
   D. The stomach

2. **With what kind of desire does the flesh deceive us?**
   A. Deadly
   B. Awesome
   C. Good
   D. Questionable

3. **According to Mark 7:21-23, where do evil things come from?**
   A. The world
   B. Satan
   C. Within us
   D. Hell

4. **Both Eve and Achin gave in to flesh appeal. Through which of the senses did the flesh initiate that appeal?**
   A. Through touch
   B. Through smell
   C. Through sight
   D. Through hearing

5. **When we trust ourselves in the flesh to desire what is good for us, what does that lead us to doubt about God?**
   A. The goodness of His desires for us
   B. His power to raise the dead
   C. His eternal nature
   D. His Lordship

6. Which of the following is the flesh NOT capable of?

A. To enslave
B. To deceive
C. To satisfy
D. All of the above

7. Which of these responses should you NOT have with the flesh?

A. Take direction from
B. Reason and argue
C. Agree
D. All of the above

8. The Israelites preferred slavery over freedom, for fear of

A. death.
B. hunger.
C. thirst.
D. all of the above.

9. What is one way to keep from being misguided by the flesh?

A. Learn to use a compass
B. Study Greek
C. Stop arguing and reasoning with yourself
D. Believe what you feel

10. What is your guide to truth?

A. What you feel
B. The Spirit
C. Your gut
D. Asking questions

What Do You Say?

"Expose" or recall a time in your life when the flesh appealed, enslaved, or deceived you. How did you find victory or hope in this circumstance?

LESSON 2

Identifying Our Flesh

The desires of the flesh are against the Spirit, and the desires of the Spirit are against the flesh, for these are opposed to each other, to keep you from doing the things you want to do.... Now the deeds of the flesh are evident, which are: immorality, impurity, sensuality, idolatry, sorcery, enmities, strife, jealousy, outbursts of anger, disputes, dissensions, factions, envying, drunkenness, carousing, and things like these. (Gal. 5:17, 19-21a)

Now that we have seen how the flesh works, we must begin identifying it in our own lives. We are often blissfully unaware of its work in our lives, and yet it may be wreaking havoc on us and those around us. We must expose the flesh in our lives in order to kill it.

Examine Yourself

Taking a close look at our flesh is uncomfortable, so we often prefer to skip ahead and instead search ourselves for evidence of the Spirit's fruit. If we can't find any, we quickly try to manufacture some of our own in an attempt to make ourselves look and feel good. We don't want to spend a lot of time digging up or rooting out the ugly mindsets and behaviors in our lives.

Our job is to crucify the flesh, leaving the Spirit to produce fruit in our lives.

Our job is not to produce spiritual fruit to try to cover over the flesh. Our job is to crucify the flesh, leaving the Spirit to produce fruit in our lives. You can only walk by the Spirit once your flesh has been put to death. And for that sinful, natural side of your flesh to die, it must be exposed.

The identity of the flesh is:

independence from God	ME-first attitude	fame
depression	anxiety	control
self-satisfaction	selfish sexual pleasure	pornography
complaining	pride	jealousy
envy	anger	rage
drunkenness	gambling	adultery
binge eating	gossiping	deceitfulness
hostility	suspicion	quarreling
controversy	being offended	holding grudges
finding fault	dividing friends	making enemies
insisting on your way	needing to be right	self-hate
refusing to accept humble positions	pleasure in inflicting pain on others or on self	trying to "out-do" someone else

Since the flesh is always in opposition to the Spirit, it manifests itself as opposite to the fruit as well. These too are evidence of the flesh:

selfishness	hate	disdain
discontentment	bitterness	not forgiving
conflict	threats	fear
revenge	irritation	cruelty
rudeness	stinginess	self-absorption
unreliability	inconsistency	negligence
giving up easily	harshness	a critical spirit
roughness	indulgence	impulsivity
gluttony	laziness	lack of discipline

Don't just examine yourself for the fruit of the Spirit; be on watch for these fruit (or works) of the flesh (Gal. 5:19-21). The flesh is the main hindrance to the Spirit's work in your spiritual life; seeing that it is alive and active can seem too disheartening, even too disgusting. The temptation to give up on identifying your flesh is exactly what the flesh wants you to do.

According to Galatians 5:22-23, the fruit produced by the Spirit is love, joy, peace, patience, kindness, goodness, faithfulness, gentleness, and self-control. We sometimes have trouble finding evidence of these good things in our lives, and strive to produce them in our own efforts. The problem is that this produces a sort of "counterfeit spirituality" that will inevitably fail.

Just because what I do seems good to me doesn't mean the Spirit produced the fruit. No amount of "good" fruit I produce can start me on a walk in the Spirit. If I look to the flesh to feel good about myself, then I have not left the flesh to walk by the Spirit. *Counterfeit spirituality* is an insidious trick of the flesh, and it can keep us "stuck," unable to move forward in our spiritual walk.

The Flesh vs. the Spirit

Consider for a moment the analogy or image of bobsledding. Two men, using all the strength in their legs, push their sled along 50 meters of an icy track to gain as much speed as possible before jumping into the sled and steering down a winding, perilous runway.

Sometimes we treat the Christian life as if it were a bobsled race. Using our own strength, we try to give ourselves a good push to godly living and assume that, at some point, we can just jump onto the Holy Spirit and He'll pick up the pace, continuing in the same direction.

You might argue, "Since you put it that way, it sounds bad, but is it really that bad to try hard? Is it wrong to make an effort? Doesn't Paul, in his letters to Timothy, tell him to 'pursue righteousness,' 'fight the good fight' (1 Tim. 6:11-12), 'be diligent to present yourself approved to God' (2 Tim. 3:15)? Doesn't God expect me to do my part first?"

I am not advocating spiritual laziness, but neither will I promote a flesh and Spirit collaboration. I am saying that what I do in the flesh, even though it seems full of good effort, will not be picked up and carried on by the Spirit. Remember what Galatians 5:17 says, that the flesh and the Spirit are constantly opposed to each other. They do not, at any time, work together towards the same goal. They cannot share the same path.

Look at the path that each is taking:

- The flesh desires to glorify me, and seeks self-satisfaction.
- The Spirit desires to glorify God, and seeks self-sacrifice.

The flesh and Spirit stand in contrast. The Spirit desires our good. The flesh is out to get us. It is constantly seeking to make us question our identity, our confidence, our very foundation.

A Shaky Foundation

A firm foundation provides sure footing, a sense of security and confidence. Without a firm foundation, you will lose your balance and reach out for something to steady yourself, something to grab on to. As a believer in Jesus Christ, my head tells me that Christ is my foundation, my confidence, and my Rock. After all, that is what His Word tells me (Ps. 62:7; Acts 4:11). But I don't always live as though that is true. Insecurity and doubt threaten me almost daily. I feel the ground shake underneath my feet. I lose my balance, and when I do, I reach out and "grab" without thinking. I'm hoping to restore my confidence, to feel strong again.

What makes you stand tall, feel "okay," or feel good about yourself? These things have probably formed the foundation of your confidence, and your sense of value. Unfortunately, this is like a foundation made of sand, and those little grains of sand continually shift.

On Christ I stand firm. He is the solid Rock beneath my feet; anything other than Him is sand. My head tells me that I am standing on that Rock, Jesus Christ, so why do my feet tell me the ground is shifting? Why do my legs feel wobbly?

Where is My Confidence?

When the foundation of my self-worth shakes as if trembling in an earthquake, I become disoriented and confused, wondering what is wrong. My automatic assumption is that the shaking of my worth comes from outside me. My instinct is to grab something solid, something strong, something that restores my sense of balance.

In comes the flesh to the rescue.

It's not the weak, ugly, bad side that comes (ugly flesh just makes me feel worse). No, only a strong, confident, powerful "me" is welcome at a time like this. And shouldn't it be that way? Shouldn't I counter a drop in self-esteem by remembering all that is good in me, all that is positive? I am in Christ after all. It's not right to think bad thoughts about myself. Right?

When there is a tremor in your self-confidence, when you feel insecure about who you are, what thoughts come to mind?

Do you ever think …

- "I could have done that better."
- "Can't they see how good I am? I'm just as good as so and so."
- "I don't want anyone to think I'm not perfect."

- "I can't stand someone not thinking well of me."
- "Why doesn't anyone recognize my abilities?"
- "I deserve to be treated better than that."
- "I'm not such a terrible person."

When we look to ourselves for confidence, we are actually welcoming the flesh to tell us who we are. It even tries to tell us who we are in Christ. Does that sound right? Can that work?

Do the thoughts listed above make your doubts disappear, or do you bounce between confident thoughts and thoughts such as these?

- "Something is wrong with me."
- "I'm not good enough."
- "I'll never be good enough."
- "I can't do anything right."
- "No one could ever love me."
- "I'm bad."
- "I always mess everything up."
- "I'm just a big failure."
- "I'm worthless."

What happened to our confidence in Christ? Who has stolen it? Was it Satan, our spouse, a co-worker, someone from church, our "best friend," that really popular person who seems to do everything right, our boyfriend or girlfriend, our roommate, our boss, our dad, our mom, our in-laws?

If it wasn't for them, we think, we could feel confident all the time, be more secure in who we are. We wouldn't have to feel as if we aren't good enough, as if we aren't doing enough. Have you ever been grateful to God for using your failures to make you into a better servant for Him, only to find yourself the next day in despair over the same failure? Discontent with your situation, do you focus on feeling good about yourself, and looking good in front of others?

Gratitude to God is the Spirit's fruit; fretting over feeling bad is from the flesh.

Gratitude to God is the Spirit's fruit; fretting over feeling bad is from the flesh. The transition from one to the other is so subtle that the switch often goes undetected. Imagine you are following a car to your destination, but in a moment of distraction you take your eyes off the car. When you look back, you assume the car in front of you is the one taking you where you planned to go. What if it isn't? What if the distraction was timed perfectly to confuse you? What if a switch was done to deceive you? What would be the outcome?

We pursue feeling good about ourselves as if we were still following Christ, when in truth, that pursuit is a leading of the flesh. *Christ did not come to earth and pay the price for our sin to boost our sense of worth, to make us feel good about ourselves.* Using our identity in Christ to bolster a positive image of ourselves is a delusion of the flesh.

The flesh does not desire victory over sin. And it definitely does not desire to carry a cross.

The flesh is only concerned with promoting *me*. In the flesh, I am drawn to think about *me*, worry about *me*, satisfy *me*, elevate and protect *me*. When I try to increase my value through self-promotion, I am being led by the desires of the flesh.

The flesh does not desire victory over sin. It does not desire identity in Christ. And it definitely does not desire to carry a cross.

Glorification by Crucifixion

In John 12, the hour for the Son of Man to be glorified had come. It was at this time that Jesus said:

> Unless a grain of wheat falls into the earth and dies, it remains by itself alone, but if it dies, it bears much fruit. He who loves his life loses it; and he who hates his life in this world shall keep it to life eternal. If anyone serves Me, let him follow Me; and where I am, there shall My servant also be; if anyone serves Me the Father will honor him. (John 12:24-26)

For Jesus Christ, that hour of glorification was death on a cross and resurrection from the grave three days later. In His day, death by crucifixion wasn't just the most painful method of execution, it was also the most humiliating. The criminal was required to carry his own crossbeam to his death. He was then hung as a spectacle, often stripped naked. This form of execution was reserved for the worst of the criminals. And this was how Jesus bore the punishment for our sin. But before He carried that crossbeam, Jesus said:

> If anyone wishes to come after Me, he must deny himself, and take up his cross daily, and follow Me. (Luke 9:23)

The hour for a decision has come. What will you do with your flesh? To walk in the Spirit, we must *crucify the flesh.* In Christ, we are freed from slavery to our flesh. But this freedom doesn't come automatically. It requires a walk of dying.

Before we can begin crucifying the flesh, we must see our flesh lose its value. We must be willing to abandon finding any significance in our flesh. Up to this point, I have been seeking to expose your flesh in its deceptive, alluring power. It is the flesh that opposes the Spirit living within you and hinders you from walking by Him. My purpose has been to lead you to this fork in the road where you must make a decision.

Will you accept a walk of dying to self in order to walk by the Spirit?

LESSON 2 EXAM

Use the exam sheet at the back of the course to complete your exam.

1. **When examining our daily life, we often would rather look for**
   A. the fruit of the Spirit.
   B. signs of a hard heart.
   C. signs of anger.
   D. signs or symptoms of a lack of love.

2. **When you see evidence of the flesh in your life, what should you do?**
   A. Cover it up
   B. Balance it with good
   C. Fix it
   D. Expose it

3. **What must you do to walk by the Spirit?**
   A. Have self-control
   B. Try to be a better person
   C. Crucify the flesh
   D. Always make good choices

4. **In which book of the Bible does Paul talk about the opposition between the flesh and the Spirit?**
   A. Galatians
   B. Ephesians
   C. Philippians
   D. James

5. **Opposition means that the flesh and the Spirit never**
   A. work together.
   B. share the same goals.
   C. go in the same direction.
   D. all of the above.

6. **The flesh opposes the Spirit**
   A. whenever Satan wants it to.
   B. when I don't get my way.
   C. most of the time.
   D. all of the time.

7. **Being in Christ means your identity is**
   A. rock solid.
   B. shifting like sand.
   C. shaking like an earthquake.
   D. blowing in the wind.

8. **When you look to yourself for confidence,**
   A. you will never go wrong in life.
   B. you are welcoming the flesh to tell you who you are.
   C. you will discover your true identity.
   D. you will be able to walk by the Spirit.

9. **In the flesh, you are drawn to**
   A. consider the desires of others first.
   B. think about yourself.
   C. think about your needs last.
   D. all of the above.

10. **Jesus said in Luke 9:23, if anyone wants to be my disciple, he must**
   A. deny himself.
   B. pick up his cross every day.
   C. follow Him.
   D. all of the above.

What Do You Say?

Take time to reflect on the lists of the identity and fruit (visible evidence) of the flesh (on page 20). Write about one that is particularly evident in your life.

LESSON 3

Dying to Self

I have been crucified with Christ. It is no longer I who live, but Christ who lives in me. And the life I now live in the flesh I live by faith in the Son of God, who loved me and gave himself for me. (Gal. 2:20)

In the first lesson, we saw some of the ways in which the flesh works, and looked at some Biblical characters who were brought down by it. In Lesson 2, we began to examine ourselves, seeking to expose the flesh in our lives, and discovered what we should do with our flesh—*crucify it.*

We must take on a walk of dying. This is not an easy task.

Our Values vs. God's Values

We all have a natural tendency to hide or fix the things we don't like about ourselves, and to promote the things we do like. While we parade the positive on stage for everyone to see, we hide the negative safely behind a curtain. At least that is what we think; but in the end, whether in front of or behind the curtain, our actions are natural and fleshly. Like the "filthy rags" of our righteous deeds, eventually our impressive acts are revealed as what they are: dull, stained, tarnished, rotting, selfish, and worthy of the dung heap (Is. 64:6; Phil. 3:8-9).

By "natural" I mean that which is of our human, physical self as distinct from the Spirit that dwells in the believer. I am not implying that all that is natural is bad, but that our natural capacity is not on par with God's divine power and is not to be relied upon for walking by the Spirit.

> But a natural man does not accept the things of the Spirit of God; for they are foolishness to him, and he cannot understand them, because they are spiritually appraised. (1 Cor. 2:14)

Paul tells us that the foolishness of God is wiser than any wisdom man thinks he has, and that the weakness of God is stronger than any strength man can muster up. When God wanted to put to shame the wise of the world, He chose to do that through the foolish of the world. When He wanted to shame the strong of the world, He chose to use the weak of the world. He has chosen what is despised, what is nothing, in order to cancel the things that exist (1 Cor. 1:25-28). Paul explains that God uses such seemingly strange methods so that no one will boast before Him (1 Cor. 1:29).

What we value is often not in line with what God values.

Humans are obsessed with assigning value to themselves, to things, and to others. The more we value something, the more effort we spend preserving, protecting, and pampering it. But what we value is often not in line with what God values.

Jars of Clay

This is shown in what Paul says to the Corinthian believers:

> But we have this treasure in jars of clay, to show that the surpassing power belongs to God and not from us. (2 Cor. 4:7)

The jar of clay is *not* the treasure; rather, the treasure is *in* the jar of clay. What does that mean? It means that God is our source of the greatest, most incredible, limitless power there is—and we are weak. That treasure is "the light of the knowledge of the glory of God in the face of Jesus Christ" (2 Cor. 4:6b). The jar of clay is our mortal flesh, our decaying bodies.

How much should we invest in the conservation and beautification of our "clay jars"? Will the time we've spent focused on making life better for our jars of clay balance with its true value?

Paul wants us to live differently. He tells us we have this treasure in jars of clay, and that truth changes everything! Because "we are afflicted in every way, but not crushed; perplexed, but not despairing; persecuted, but not forsaken; struck down, but not destroyed" (2 Cor. 4:8-9).

This jar of clay has no value apart from Christ. I am dead and dying, made alive only by the treasure of the light of the Gospel of the glory of Christ in me. That treasure cannot be crushed, it cannot be destroyed, and it is the only thing that matters. What happens to this jar shouldn't make any difference.

Living to Die or Dying to Live

Paul lived out this truth in his own life. While chained up in prison, he said his earnest hope was:

> That with all boldness, Christ will even now, as always, be exalted in my body, whether by life or by death. For to me, to live is Christ, and to die is gain. But if I am to live on in the flesh, this will mean fruitful labor for me; and I don't know which to choose. But I am hard-pressed from both directions, having the desire to depart and be with Christ, for that is very much better; yet to remain on in the flesh is more necessary for your sake. Convinced of this, I know that I will remain and continue with you all for your progress and joy in the faith. (Phil. 1:20-25)

Think about what Paul is writing here. He is in prison and he doesn't know which to choose: to live or to die. How difficult of a choice is that? Wouldn't it be natural for us to prefer to live? But then, if I were in prison, I probably would rather die. I, of course, would choose based on what was best for *me*. Not Paul! His primary desire is not for his own good (which for him would mean to die and be with Christ), but for the good of others and for the preaching of the Gospel.

Living by the Spirit requires a mindset that is "upside down" to our natural selves.

Living by the Spirit requires a mindset that is "upside down" to our natural selves. Obeying Jesus' teachings will go against everything that is natural to us. It is unnatural for us to ask for help, to admit we are wrong, to turn the other cheek, to love our enemies, to do good to them, to submit to others, to give thanks in all things, to suffer, to be weak, to surrender our rights, to love mercy, to be faithful, to pray, to be humble, to be content, to seek unity, or to accept slavery.

Paul instructs us to "put on the Lord Jesus Christ and make no provision for the flesh in regard to its lusts" (Rom. 13:14). What does it mean to "put on the Lord Jesus Christ"? Do I wear what He wore, do what He did, act as He acted? *How do I walk His walk?* Remember that Jesus said,

> If anyone wishes to come after Me, he must deny himself, and take up his cross daily, and follow Me. (Luke 9:23)

The criminal condemned to die by crucifixion had to carry his own cross, demonstrating that he was going to his death. He was a "dead man walking." Jesus wants those who follow Him to walk in the Spirit with a cross on their back.

Paul says that death has already occurred in the believer: "Knowing this, that our old self was crucified with Him…" (Rom. 6:6a) and "Those who belong to Christ Jesus have crucified the flesh with its passions and desires" (Gal. 5:24). He also says that we have an active role in putting to death whatever belongs to our earthly nature, replacing it with compassion, kindness, humility, gentleness, meekness, patience, tolerance, forgiveness, and, above all, *love*, the glue that holds us all together in harmony. We must also rid ourselves of such things as anger, rage, malice, slander, filthy language, and lying (Col. 3:5-14).

Paul understood that to walk by the Spirit, the natural man has to die. He lived taking up the cross of Jesus every day, and was willing to look foolish (in the world's eyes) to do so. If our goal is to walk by the Spirit and die daily, we would do well to learn from Paul.

> Always carrying about in the body the dying of Jesus, so that the life of Jesus also may be manifested in our body. For we who live are constantly being delivered over to death for Jesus's sake, so that the life of Jesus also may be manifested in our mortal flesh. (2 Cor. 4:10-11)

We can't explain it, can't understand it, can't grasp it—We only know that this is true: two opposite realities co-exist in us, both the *dying* and the *life* of Jesus at the same time. That should radically change the way we live. For Jesus' sake, for His purpose, for His glory, for His name, we live to be constantly handed over to death. We carry in this body the dying of Jesus, so that His life will be seen in us. We live to die so that the real living is Jesus in us.

The Difficulty of Dying to Self

Each year, I grow more and more convinced that, to live by the Spirit, I must crucify the flesh. I've tried to avoid it and find another way, but each time I find myself defeated yet again. The only solution is to constantly be *dying to self.* I must daily consider my flesh dead, daily carry around the death of Christ in my body. Every day I wake up with a death sentence; I am a dead man walking. I've never known a more persistent and proud enemy than my own flesh. It wants nothing to do with death. It kicks and screams its way to the executioner. And just when I think I've slain the beast, it rises again. Perhaps you have had the same experience.

Crucifying the flesh is not natural! Without the Spirit, we cannot begin to choose to die to self today, and tomorrow, and the day after that. The good news is that—unlike the man who has been sentenced to death, who walks the hall to his execution with no hope—we have hope. Our death sentence carries the certainty of life. We are dead to sin, but alive in Christ.

Two opposite realities co-exist in us, both the dying and the life of Jesus at the same time.

So, how do you die to self? That is *the* question, and we can be tempted to come up with some easy steps on how to do this on our own. This is a mistake. This would be viewing dying to self as something *we* do.

That's the wrong approach. God hasn't left us in charge of the dying process. In His Word, we learn of four effective methods that *He* has designed and put in place. The answer to the question, "How do I die to self?" is not found in what *we* do, but in surrendering to *God's* use of these methods.

The next section describes in detail God's four step method to dying to self: weakness, suffering, humility, and repentance.

LESSON 3 EXAM

Use the exam sheet at the back of the course to complete your exam.

1. **What can we rely on for walking by the Spirit?**
   A. Our natural abilities
   B. Our physical strength
   C. Our righteous deeds
   D. The indwelling Spirit

2. **According to 1 Corinthians 1:25-29, why has God chosen the weak and foolish to shame the wise and strong?**
   A. Because all men are fools
   B. So the weak and foolish could now boast in themselves
   C. So that Christians can look smarter
   D. So that no one can boast before God

3. **What do we typically not do to the things we value most?**
   A. Pamper
   B. Protect
   C. Mistreat
   D. Preserve

4. **Paul refers to our bodies as "jars of clay," or "earthen vessels," and contrasts that with a treasure inside. According to 2 Corinthians 4:7, what is the reason for the contrast?**
   A. To give us a treasure map
   B. To help us feel better about ourselves
   C. To showcase God's great power and our weakness
   D. To stop us from complaining

5. **Paul writes from prison that**
   A. he wishes he could be released.
   B. he knows the Lord will release him.
   C. he's not sure whether he'd want to live or die.
   D. that he lives with regrets about his past choices.

6. **In the life of a believer,**
   A. the flesh needs to be put to death through the Spirit.
   B. the flesh isn't a problem.
   C. the flesh has already been put to death.
   D. Both A and C.

7. **What has happened to our old self?**
   A. It has been crucified with Christ
   B. It is waiting to be remade.
   C. It is becoming more like Christ.
   D. It is sleeping.

8. **What two opposite realities co-exist in the believer?**
   A. Darkness and light
   B. The dying and life of Jesus
   C. The old cloth and the new cloth
   D. A good angel and a bad angel

9. **Dying to self is**
   A. something I do.
   B. something God takes charge of.
   C. takes three easy steps.
   D. a one time thing.

10. **What Biblical methods of dying to self are presented in this lesson?**
   A. Going to church, reading my Bible, praying every day
   B. Evangelizing, making disciples, mission trips
   C. Making a wooden cross and carrying it
   D. Weakness, suffering, humility, and repentance

What Do You Say?

Is dying to self, or crucifying the flesh, a new concept to you? Explain.

LESSON 4

Weakness

And I was with you in weakness and in fear and much trembling, and my speech and my message were not in plausible words of wisdom, but in demonstration of the Spirit and of power, so that your faith might not rest in the wisdom of men but in the power of God. (1 Cor. 2:3-5, ESV)

I hate being weak. I want to believe that I can do anything. My working premise is that I should be strong enough, that I should be able to just cancel weakness with determination. Does this work? Not usually, but I keep thinking it will.

Do you do this too? Do you tell yourself, "I should be strong enough to do this"? The problem isn't that we think we are strong; most of us know we're not. The problem is that we think we *should* be strong.

Keeping this delusion of strength alive prevents us from learning God's purpose for weakness. Telling ourselves that we can be strong, that we should be strong, gives us just enough strength to keep from dying to self. Every time we hope to find strength in ourselves, we miss the true power of weakness.

Weakness Is Good?

I think of weakness as a place we go to unintentionally. When we "arrive" at Weakness (speaking figuratively), not only are we disappointed that we didn't arrive where we wanted to, we're also frustrated because we were trying to avoid this place. "Why am I here again? I don't want to be here!" we exclaim. We feel angry, afraid, trapped, and hopeless. There is something suffocating about weakness that makes us feel desperate. We're embarrassed at having come to Weakness despite our efforts to avoid it. Nothing is going the way we want, and we can't make sense of our failure to do anything about it. We refuse to accept our failure to be strong, disturbed by the thought that others will think we're weak and get the wrong impression of us. We hate being reminded that we are weak when others correct us, when our failures, mistakes, and bad choices make our weaknesses public. So we conclude that anything that makes us feel weak is bad and must be avoided.

What if weakness was entirely different? What if weakness was good? What if it was better than strength?

None of us are good at everything, but sometimes we would like to think we can be. Ashamed when others discover our inadequacies, we cover our weaknesses. We work hard at appearing strong, at hiding our emotions, at building walls. When the flesh takes charge of weakness, it makes us forget that we are dead men walking. The flesh insists that we are too strong to die, even when we feel drained of all strength.

Look at what Paul says:

> And I was with you in weakness and in fear and much trembling, and my speech and my message were not in plausible words of wisdom, but in demonstration of the Spirit and of power. (1 Cor. 2:3-4, ESV)

When the Spirit takes over our weakness, something amazing happens. God comes in and accomplishes things we never dreamed were possible. We are awed by His greatness and humbled by our smallness. We are no longer dismayed by our inadequacy. We no longer compare ourselves to God or resent Him for His strength. Instead, we are grateful for our limitations, realizing that without them we could never know God's creative power in our lives.

Weakness says power from God.

Brag About Weakness

If we were living by the Spirit, we would say with Paul, "if I have to brag, then I will brag about everything that makes me look weak."

> If I have to boast, I will boast of what pertains to my weakness. (2 Cor. 11:30)

Does that sound ridiculous or backwards? Yes, but we should be used to that. Nothing about walking in the Spirit makes sense to our natural selves. In the flesh, we're too proud to be weak. In the Spirit, we will talk about our weaknesses as if we were proud of them—not to bring glory to ourselves, but to bring glory to God.

Paul's 180° approach to weakness, however, must dramatically change how we see and react to weakness. To boast in our weaknesses means we are no longer ashamed of them, no longer frustrated, angered, or discouraged by them. It means that we no longer hate what makes us feel weak. To boast in our weaknesses is to stop taking pride in our strengths, and, instead, to take pride in our weaknesses.

Think about the things you want others to see you doing, the things you secretly hope will gain you a reputation of brilliance, the things that make you feel superior, the great things you've accomplished. If you could, you would brag about them a little. Maybe you do.

Now think about your weaknesses in the same way. Rather than making you inferior, your weaknesses commend you to greatness in the Lord. Rather than causing shame, they glorify God. Don't hate them; rejoice in them.

Boasting in our weaknesses saps power from the flesh, causing it to die a little more, taking us one step closer to living by the Spirit.

> My grace is sufficient for you, for my power is made perfect in weakness. (2 Cor. 12:9)

It started with Paul's desperate pleas to be rid of his "thorn in the flesh" (1 Cor. 12:7) when those words came as a reply from the Lord. I wonder how long it took for those words to take root and flourish in Paul's heart. How long did it take before he could say this with all confidence:

> Therefore, I will boast all the more gladly of my weaknesses, so that the power of Christ may rest upon me. For the sake of Christ, then, I am content with weaknesses, insults, hardships, persecutions, and calamities. For when I am weak, then I am strong. (2 Cor. 12:9b-10)

That the apostle Paul could say that he will, with all gladness, take pride in his weaknesses seems ridiculous. He says he is well-pleased, content with weaknesses, insults, distresses, persecutions, and calamities! What could make Paul be happy with this? Let's take another look at a paraphrase of what the Lord said to him.

> *My* grace is enough to satisfy, to make you content, *My* miraculous power and deeds are fulfilled in the weakness that keeps you from being able to accomplish what you want.

Are you willing to exchange pride in your own fulfillment for joy in His?

The flesh cannot take pleasure in weakness because its only desire is self-fulfillment. If we keep walking in the flesh and looking at weakness from our perspective, we will only see what keeps us from being independent, from being able to do what we want, from being good enough.

In the Spirit, weakness is where God takes what *we can't do* to do what only *He can*. When we are pleased in our weaknesses, He is most glorified and we are most satisfied.

Jesus Knows our Weakness

The beauty of accepting God's use of weakness to bring about the death of your flesh is the promise of the life of Jesus that accompanies it. In the living Jesus, we have all that we need to endure weakness. In the living Jesus, we have the most perfect One who understands all our weaknesses.

> For we do not have a high priest who cannot sympathize with our weaknesses. (Hebrews 4:15a)

Sympathesai, the Greek word that describes what Jesus our High Priest does for us, means more than just to sympathize. It means that He "fellow-feels" with us. It means that He is affected by the same feelings that affect us.

What a difference it makes to talk to others who are able to feel what you feel! You can see it in their eyes, hear it in their voice, and you know that they know. You feel comforted, feel that you're not alone, feel that there is hope.

Jesus, Our High Priest, is full of compassion, understands all our weaknesses, and never loses His patience with us—even when we act foolishly. He loads us up with all the grace and mercy we could ever need, especially when we have nothing left.

Soul Anchor of Hope

When I began writing on weakness, I planned to include something about our High Priest understanding our weaknesses, but I never expected to spend so much time in Hebrews. When I tried to pull that one strand out, I couldn't separate it from the rest of the letter.

Hebrews tells us that Jesus is a priest according to the order of Melchizedek. What does that mean? It means that He is a priest forever, and it means that His priesthood came with an oath God swore by Himself, because He could swear by no one greater.

> The Lord has sworn and will not change His mind, "You are a priest forever." (Heb. 7:21)

You may think, "that's nice, but I'm not sure why that is important to me." It's like this: life has a way of tossing you about like a small boat on the ocean. You need an anchor to keep you from being bounced about. This Melchizedekian priesthood comes with a hope the size and weight of an anchor—not at all like that thin, fragile hope that keeps us holding on to something or someone that isn't even good for us.

Jesus, Our High Priest, is full of compassion, and understands all our weaknesses.

This anchor comes with a High Priest that lives forever. This anchor comes with a promise, an oath, from God that He will never leave you, never give up on you. And God doesn't lie or change His mind.

Read and decide for yourself:

> In the same way God, desiring even more to show to the heirs of the promise the unchangeableness of His purpose, interposed with an oath, so that by two unchangeable things, in which it is impossible for God to lie, we who have taken refuge would have strong encouragement to take hold of the hope set before us. This hope we have as an anchor of the soul, a hope both sure and steadfast and one which enters within the veil, where Jesus has entered as a forerunner for us, having become a high priest forever according to the order of Melchizedek. (Heb. 6:17-20)

> Who has become such not on the basis of a law of physical requirement, but according to the power of an indestructible life. (Heb. 7:16)

What's more, previous priests were always being replaced because they died, but Jesus,

> Because He continues forever, holds His priesthood permanently. Therefore He is able to save forever those who draw near to God through Him, since He always lives to make intercession for them. (Heb. 7:24-25)

Jesus Christ, Our High Priest, gives us free and confident access to the presence of God, access He bought for us with His own blood through the sacrifice of His own body. With Him, where He has gone right up to heaven, we have a hope so sure and trustworthy it is an anchor for our soul. How beautiful for a soul, caught in a raging storm, to find himself or herself secured to an anchor that will not budge! What soul, blinded and confused by insecurities, unreliable relationships, disappointments, illnesses, and lost jobs, doesn't long for such a hope!

As you embrace weakness, the hope of eternal life in Christ is your soul anchor.

Because Jesus lives forever, He saves forever. Because He lives, He intercedes for me, forever and always. His life is indestructible; therefore, my hope is indestructible!

The Lord designs trials to reveal our weaknesses, which in turn, builds our endurance. That cross on our back will make us wobbly, it will make us weak, it will feel like suffering, it will humble us. That is what we can expect when we walk by the Spirit in weakness. If you haven't experienced this yet, you will, and, when you do, you will want an anchor.

As you embrace weakness, the hope of eternal life in Christ is your soul anchor.

LESSON 4 EXAM

Use the exam sheet at the back of the course to complete your exam.

1. When looking at weakness through the flesh, what are we most likely going to conclude?

A. Weakness is bad
B. Weakness should be avoided
C. Weakness is discouraging
D. All of the above

2. As a tool in God's hands, what does weakness NOT do for the believer?

A. Perfect God's power in the believer
B. Make the believer humble
C. Make the believer invincible
D. Help the believer die to self and live by the Spirit

3. What does weakness say in the Spirit?

A. You're not good enough
B. You are stronger than that
C. It's not my fault
D. Power from God

4. In 2 Corinthians 11:30, what does Paul say he would boast about?

A. His visions
B. His endurance
C. His weakness
D. His strength

5. According to 2 Corinthians 12:9b, for what purpose did Paul conclude that he would rather boast in his weaknesses?

A. So that the power of Christ would dwell in him
B. So that others would think he was humble
C. So that he could win Gentiles for Christ
D. So that he could feel better about himself

6. What does it mean that Jesus our High Priest can "sympathesai" with us?

A. He can no longer sympathize with us.
B. He feels sorry for us.
C. He will pray for us.
D. He feels what we feel.

7. What does it mean that Jesus' priesthood comes from the order of Melchizedek?

A. His priesthood lasts forever.
B. Melchizedek is his father.
C. He is a very old priest.
D. His priesthood wears long brown robes.

8. How does the author of Hebrews describe this hope we have in Jesus?

A. As a rock
B. As an unsure thing
C. As an anchor for the soul
D. As a balloon

9. According to Hebrews, which statement is true about the priesthood of Jesus?

A. It is permanent and indestructible.
B. His power to save is eternal.
C. He will never stop interceding for us with the Father.
D. All of the above.

10. The Lord designs trials

A. because he is unkind and unjust.
B. to help us trust in our own strength.
C. to crush us.
D. to reveal our weaknesses and build our endurance.

What Do You Say?

What impresses you about having Jesus Christ as your High Priest?

____

____

____

____

LESSON 5

Suffering

For to you it has been granted for Christ's sake, not only to believe in Him, but also to suffer for His sake. (Phil. 1:29)

To walk by the Spirit, we must put the flesh to death. God allows suffering in our lives to accomplish that death. Suffering is guaranteed; the choice before us is whether to suffer *our* way in the flesh, or to suffer *God's* way in the Spirit.

Suffering vs. Surrender

First of all, let's talk about *counterfeit suffering.* Our flesh likes to deceive us in redefining what true suffering is, confusing *suffering* and *surrender.*

Webster's dictionary defines suffering as "being forced to endure pain, inconvenience or loss."[1] The feeling of pain, inconvenience, or loss depends heavily on how much we refuse to surrender, and on what we feel we have a right to have. For example, the world says, "it's your right to be happy." Therefore, if your marriage makes you unhappy, the world says you should leave it. Advertisements say we deserve the latest trends or newest electronics. Society tells us that we have a right to a bigger house and a more comfortable lifestyle. The flesh tells us that we have a right to achieve our dreams, to be treated well, to take revenge, to be satisfied, or to do whatever makes us feel good.

Our flesh likes to deceive us in redefining what true suffering is.

Being denied what we think is rightfully ours—this is counterfeit suffering. It is a subtle, but effective, trick of the flesh. The concept of *rights* creates a false sense of loss, which then creates an illusion of suffering. Our basic "right to be happy" can, by itself, bring us into a place of "suffering" where we don't belong.

Suffering is God's tool to crucify the flesh, but that crucifixion won't happen as long as we believe that sacrificing the things we have or wish we had, or feel we have a right to have, is true suffering. The first step to authentic suffering in the Spirit, then, is surrendering the right to choose how we will suffer, and agreeing to the Lord's terms. When we do this, a lot of what we think of as suffering evaporates, and what's left is a beautiful, countercultural suffering—suffering that brings joy.

Unfair Suffering

Another way the flesh tries to redefine suffering in our minds is to call it *unfair*. It causes us to ask, "How can a loving God allow so much suffering in the world?" Our issue isn't so much with suffering, as it is with who suffers. We find it incomprehensible that God allows suffering to come to good people who don't deserve it! We don't trust Him to be just.

While walking on the beach after His resurrection, Jesus reveals to Peter that his death will involve some suffering. Peter does what I would: he looks back at that other disciple John, and asks, "What about him?" (John 21:21b).

We naturally balance reward with behavior. Naturally that is the right way the universe should work. What about suffering? Should that be balanced too? Does it seem unfair when you suffer more than others?

Suffering in the Spirit is impossible without a love of God's grace.

The idea of fairness is flesh-based, and undermines our belief in God's justice. To suffer in the Spirit, you have to know that God is just and trust Him to act justly. We will not arrive at the right perspective on suffering if we start with the false premise that we or the universe (i.e., karma) can be more just than the Creator, our heavenly Father. To associate suffering or reward with past or present behavior is to invite God's judgment without His mercy, without His grace.

We can only suffer according to the will of God if we are completely surrendered to His justice, a justice that secured forgiveness of sin for us, even though every molecule of our flesh is wretchedly undeserving.

God's choice doesn't depend on the will or actions of man, but on God who has mercy. Does the created thing say to its creator, "Why have you made me this way?" The potter has the right to make something common or make something rare out of the same piece of clay. Although willing and right to show His power by destroying vessels of wrath, God acts justly when, through great patience, He holds back His wrath and shows the great riches of His glory on vessels of mercy. Our Lord is righteous in all He does. He is also richly merciful to the unrighteous (Rom. 9:20-23).

We are not paid according to our deeds. God offers forgiveness to the wicked, forgiveness that is totally undeserved. It is not a justice that we would consider right and fair, but it is justice according to God.

Suffering in the Spirit is impossible without a love of God's grace. If we insist on judging others for their works, on expecting God to judge others according to their works, then we invite Him to deal with us in the same way.

Suffering for Doing Good

We cheer when the wicked suffer, perhaps even tolerate our own suffering when we know that we brought it on ourselves, but we can't understand suffering that accompanies doing good. Peter wrote about this relationship between suffering and doing good.

> When you do what is right and suffer for it, you patiently endure it, this finds favor with God. For you have been called for this purpose, since Christ also suffered for you, leaving you an example for you to follow in His steps. (1 Peter 2:20b-21)

> But even if you should suffer for the sake of righteousness, you are blessed.... For it is better, if God should will it so, that you suffer for doing what is right rather than for doing what is wrong. (1 Peter 3:14, 17)

> Beloved, do not be surprised at the fiery ordeal among you, which comes upon you for your testing, as though some strange thing were happening to you; but to the degree that you share the sufferings of Christ, keep on rejoicing; so that also at the revelation of His glory, you may rejoice with exultation....
>
> If you are reviled for the name of Christ, you are blessed, because the Spirit of glory and of God rests upon you. Make sure that none of you suffer as a murderer, or thief, or evildoer, or a troublesome meddler; but if anyone suffers as a Christian, he is not to be ashamed, but is to glorify God in that name....

> Therefore, those also who suffer according to the will of God shall entrust their souls to a faithful Creator in doing what is right. (1 Peter 4:12-13, 14-16, 19)

Don't stop doing good, even when you suffer for it. Remember that you are entrusting yourself to your faithful Lord, not to anyone else. The truth of God's Word is not that we are to do good to avoid suffering, but that we are to do good in the midst of suffering.

Don't stop doing good, even when you suffer for it.

Suffering and the Word

The Psalmist said, "It is good for me that I was afflicted, that I may learn your statutes" (Ps. 119:71). Suffering drives us to the Word. The Word strengthens us in suffering. They are mutually dependent.

Psalm 119 is full of encouragement, telling us what God's Word does for us in the midst of suffering.

> My soul weeps because of grief; strengthen me according to your word. (119:28)

> This is my comfort in my affliction, that your word has revived me. (119:50)

> The cords of the wicked have encircled me, but I have not forgotten your law. (119:61)

> It is good for me that I was afflicted, that I may learn your statutes. (119:71)

> I know, O Lord, that your judgments are righteous, and that in faithfulness you have afflicted me. (119:75)

> If your law had not been my delight, then I would have perished in my affliction. (119:92)

> I will never forget your precepts, for by them You have revived me. (119:93)

> I am exceedingly afflicted, revive me, O Lord, according to your word. (119:107)

> I know, O Lord, that your regulations are fair, you disciplined me because I needed it. Now let your unfailing love comfort me, just as you promised me, your servant. Surround me with your tender mercies so I may live, for your instructions are my delight. (119:75-76, NLT)

> Your eternal word, O Lord, stands firm in heaven. Your faithfulness extends to every generation, as enduring as the earth You created. Your regulations remain true to this day, for everything serves your plans. If your instructions hadn't sustained me with joy, I would have died in my misery. I will never forget your commandments, for by them you give me life. (119:89-93, NLT)

God's Word, eternal and faithful, sustains us and restores our joy in suffering. The flesh will never prompt you to read God's word; therefore, counterfeit suffering can never produce joy.

Suffering and Purpose

Does God have a purpose for your life? What if that purpose was to suffer? I admit it sounds masochistic, but accepting suffering is only perverse if you are getting fleshly pleasure out of it. That's not the purpose Peter had in mind when he said,

> You have been called for this purpose, since Christ also suffered for you, leaving you an example for you to follow in His steps. (1 Peter 2:21)

What purpose could suffering have in your life? First, it is your best weapon against sin.

> Therefore since Christ has suffered in the flesh, arm yourselves also with the same purpose, because he who has suffered in the flesh has ceased from sin. (1 Peter 4:1)

Second, it makes you better. You are promised that,

> After you have suffered for a little while, the God of all grace, who called you to His eternal glory in Christ, will Himself, perfect, confirm, strengthen and establish you. (1 Peter 5:10)

Last, consider Jesus' words:

> "Truly, truly, I say to you, unless a grain of wheat falls into the earth and dies, it remains alone; but if it dies, it bears much fruit. Whoever loves his life loses it, and whoever hates his life in this world will keep it for eternal life. If anyone serves me, he must follow me; and where I am, there will my servant be also. If anyone serves me, the Father will honor him. Now is my soul troubled. And what shall I say? 'Father, save me from this hour'? But for this purpose I have come to this hour. Father, glorify your name." Then a voice came from heaven: "I have glorified it, and I will glorify it again." (John 12:24-28a, ESV)

Suffering helps me to my death. That doesn't give me purpose; it is my purpose. What should I say, then, in response to pain and suffering, "Father, deliver me?" No. Instead, I should say, "Father be glorified!"

> When through fiery trials your pathway shall lie,
> My grace, all-sufficient, shall be your supply;
> The flame shall not hurt you; I only design
> Your dross to consume, and your gold to refine.[2]

LESSON 5 EXAM

Use the exam sheet at the back of the course to complete your exam.

1. **What must we do to walk by the Spirit?**
   A. Follow a set of rules to keep us from sin
   B. Put to death the flesh
   C. Work hard to be better Christians
   D. Avoid suffering

2. **What is one tool God uses to put to death our flesh?**
   A. Suffering
   B. Self-awareness
   C. Fulfilled longings
   D. Instant gratification

3. **The idea of fairness**
   A. is flesh-based.
   B. represents God's grace.
   C. is promoted by the Spirit.
   D. all of the above.

4. **What attitude makes suffering difficult to accept?**
   A. The belief that doing good is rewarded with good.
   B. The belief that things should be fair.
   C. The belief that God is unjust.
   D. All of the above.

5. **God's choice regarding suffering depends on**
   A. our surrender.
   B. our present behavior.
   C. our stubbornness.
   D. God, who has mercy.

6. **Suffering in the Spirit is impossible**
   A. when you think you deserve better.
   B. without a love of God's grace.
   C. when you demand your rights.
   D. all of the above.

7. What should we never stop doing in the midst of suffering?

A. Crying
B. Complaining
C. Good
D. Singing

8. If we are suffering in the Spirit, suffering will

A. drive us to the Word of God.
B. never produce joy.
C. always be a consequence of our sin.
D. cause us to do evil.

9. What is one purpose for suffering in the life of a believer?

A. To pay for past sins
B. To arm us against sin
C. To make us miserable
D. To shorten our lives

10. When facing the suffering of the cross, how did Jesus Christ pray?

A. "Make this happen as quickly as possible."
B. "Can I get a little help here?"
C. "Help me keep my dignity."
D. "Father, glorify your name."

What Do You Say?

Have you ever gone through a time of suffering? After reading this lesson, what purpose do you think it had in your life?

___

___

___

___

LESSON 6

Humility

He laid aside his outer garments, and taking a towel, tied it around his waist. Then he poured water into a basin and began to wash the disciples' feet. (John 13:4-5)

To follow Christ is to take up your cross daily, to crucify the flesh, to die to self. Of the four tools God uses to help us die to self, we have talked about two: weakness and suffering. The next two tools, humility and repentance, require radical changes of heart. These two go straight for the jugular of our flesh, that is, our pride and sin.

You know your pride needs humility when …

- you insist on being right.
- you want to prove that you are better than someone else.
- you compare yourself with others.
- you try to put another down.
- you need to show off.
- you refuse to give up your rights.
- you think of yourself as better than those you serve.
- you want revenge.
- you resent those who do better than you.

You need to assume humility when …

- you are falsely accused.
- someone less qualified than you is promoted.
- you are overlooked, not appreciated, not recognized.

You need humility to …

- wait in silence.
- worship God.
- pray.

Parable of the Guests

A Pharisee invited Jesus to dinner on the Sabbath. The Pharisee then paraded a sick man in front of Jesus to see if He would break the Law and heal him. All were watching Jesus closely. They didn't realize that He was also watching them and had noticed that the dinner guests were picking places of honor. So after He healed the man, Jesus told them this parable.

> When you are invited by someone to a wedding feast, do not take the place of honor, for someone more distinguished than you may have been invited by him, and he who invited you both will come and say to you, 'Give your place to this man,' and then in disgrace you proceed to occupy the last place. But when you are invited, go and recline at the last place, so that when the one who has invited you comes, he may say to you, 'Friend, move up higher'; then you will have honor in the sight of all who are at the table with you. For everyone who exalts himself will be humbled, and he who humbles himself will be exalted. (Luke 14:11)

Then Jesus turned to the host who had invited a room full of self-important people.

When you throw a party, He said, don't invite friends, relatives, rich neighbors, and dignitaries. Don't invite people who can repay you; instead, invite the poor, crippled, blind, and lame. In other words, invite the lowest of society, the ones who can't repay you, that way you will be repaid in the resurrection.

The guests were too high in their estimation of themselves. The host sought too much exaltation from the guests he chose to invite.[1]

The foundation of our self-worth is rich soil for the roots of pride. Anything that gives you value outside of Christ provides another place for pride to put its roots. The more things you rely on for your self-worth, the more invasive is your pride.

Down Is the New Up

In whose eyes do you want to be seen as elevated? Does God take note of your elevation? Is it possible to be elevated in God's eyes?

It is, but not by going in the direction you might imagine. Jesus showed us a different way. He showed us that in God's eyes, *you move up by going down.*

> Then Jesus told this story to some who had great confidence in their own righteousness and scorned everyone else: "Two men went to the Temple to pray. One was a Pharisee, and the other was a despised tax collector. The Pharisee stood by himself and prayed this prayer: 'I thank you, God, that I am not like other people—cheaters, sinners, adulterers. I'm certainly not like that tax collector! I fast twice a week, and I give you a tenth of my income.'
>
> But the tax collector stood at a distance and dared not even lift his eyes to heaven as he prayed. Instead, he beat his chest in sorrow, saying, 'O God, be merciful to me, for I am a sinner.'
>
> I tell you, this sinner, not the Pharisee, returned home justified before God. For those who exalt themselves will be humbled, and those who humble themselves will be exalted." (Luke 18:9-14 NLT)

The proud man thinks himself in right standing with people and God. He sees himself higher than some and scorns those who are lower.

The humble man sees himself a sinner, unworthy of standing before God. He bows low to the ground, where he cannot compare his position with that of others. His humility comes from within, not from his status among other people.

When God humbles us, our first reaction is to inflate ourselves so that we will rise up, if only a few inches. This need to boost ourselves is an automatic reaction to the downward pull of humility. The problem is that what humbles us does not always make us humble. We are not content to stay down.

> Do not hold your faith in our glorious Lord Jesus Christ with an attitude of personal favoritism. For if a man comes into your assembly with a gold ring and dressed in fine clothes, and there also comes in a poor man in dirty clothes, and you pay special attention to the one who is wearing the fine clothes, and say, 'you sit here in a good place', and you say to the poor man, 'you stand over there, or sit down by my footstool', have you not made distinctions among yourselves, and become judges with evil motives? (James 2:1-4)

Seeking to elevate either myself or others is a dangerous game of arrogance, requiring an attitude of superiority, and, according to James, it is pure evil. Any attempt to elevate myself or others forces someone else to a lower position. To make some into celebrities inevitably makes others into peasants. This does not glorify God! It assigns a value, a glory to another. That is idolatry.

If you are looking down on anyone, you have put yourself higher than the Lord would have you be. The Lord says that, if you want to be great, you have to lower yourself to serve; if you want to be exalted, go from low to the lowest.

The Pride of Job

The story of Job in the Bible is told in a series of painful speeches between him and some friends who have come to offer comfort (though it's hard to see that "comfort" was their true purpose). They argued that Job must have done something bad, that his current suffering revealed wickedness beneath his apparent righteous behavior. Their arguments provoked defensiveness in Job. He could produce plenty of examples of men much more wicked than himself, living blissful lives, thereby proving the friends wrong.

As long as we seek to elevate our own worth, we cannot worship God.

Job doesn't curse God (though his wife encouraged him to do so), but you get the feeling that he had a few choice things to say, if he could just get an audience with God. In his final passionate defense, Job described the position he used to have in the community, when he would go out to the gate of the city where the important people gathered. Here the young men would step back, the old men would stand up, and princes would stop talking, putting their hands over their mouths. A hush would descend on the group when Job arrived, as if their tongues were stuck to the roofs of their mouths. Job said, "To me they listened and waited and kept silent for my counsel" (Job 29:21). But now, Job was humiliated, now young men mocked him, the sons of men that Job would not have considered worthy to mingle with his sheep dogs. They taunted him and made fun of him. He had become one who was despised, one whose condition was so disgusting that no one came near him except to spit on him. Job was humbled and afflicted.[2] Looking up at the height of his former glory made his fall harder, and the distance of his fall more painful.

Then the Lord spoke out of a whirlwind, and Job finally stopped talking:

> I am unworthy, how can I reply to you? I put my hand over my mouth. (Job 40:4, NIV)

Job's problem was his pride that surfaced in his suffering. Through all his suffering, he wouldn't stop defending his exalted self, wouldn't stop seeing himself as a man worthy of commanding silence from those around him. Despite the extreme physical humiliation he suffered, Job had been caught in the current of his pride, swirling in the pool of his own significance, because he had not lowered his spirit to match his circumstances. He had not yet been humbled.

Pride is idolatry. Pride seeks worship. It hates being brought down from its lofty place. As long as we seek to elevate our own worth, we cannot worship God.

Pulverized in His Presence

Isaiah 66:2 gives us an indication of how we should approach our Creator: humble, contrite, and trembling.

The Hebrew word for *contrite* (Ps. 51:17, Isa. 57:15) means "to be crushed to powder, or pulverized."

We cannot gain humility through our efforts; rather, we gain humility by emptying ourselves. We cannot be humble without being emptied and crushed. If we think we have something to offer to God, even if that thing is our humility, we are not yet humble.

> For though the Lord is exalted, yet He regards the lowly; but the haughty He knows from afar. (Ps. 138:6)

> Crawl into caves in the rocks. Hide in the dust from the terror of the Lord and the glory of His majesty. Human pride will be brought down, And human arrogance will be humbled. Only the Lord will be exalted on that day of judgment. (Isa. 2:10-11, NLT)

> Thus says the Lord, "Heaven is my throne, and the earth is my footstool, where then is a house you could build for me. And where is a place that I may rest? For my hand made all these things, thus all these things came into being," declares the Lord. "But to this one I will look, to him who is humble and contrite of spirit, who trembles at my word." (Isa. 66:1-2)

> On that day you will no longer need to be ashamed, for you will no longer be rebels against me. I will remove all proud and arrogant people from among you. There will be no more haughtiness on my holy mountain. Those who are left will be the lowly and humble, for it is they who trust in the name of the Lord. (Zeph. 3:11-12, NLT)

> God is opposed to the proud but gives grace to the humble … humble yourselves in the presence of the Lord and He will exalt you. (James 4:6, 10)

According to these verses, what does our pride get us? It puts us in opposition to God, it gets us far from Him, and it gets us banished from His holy mountain.

Only the lowly will be with Him in that high place, only the contrite will dwell in His presence, only the humble will call Him Holy.

The Humility of Jesus

Jesus is the ultimate example of dying to self. Paul points to His example of extreme humility as what we should imitate.

> Have this attitude in yourselves which was also in Christ Jesus, who, although He existed in the form of God, did not regard equality with God a thing to be grasped, but emptied Himself, taking the form of a bond-servant, and being made in the likeness of men. Being found in appearance as a man, He humbled Himself by becoming obedient to the point of death, even death on a cross. (Phil. 2:5-8)

Jesus, the glorious Creator of all things, humbled Himself to live with His lowly creation. He was unjustly accused, and yet did not respond in retaliation. Though He was powerful enough to stop His humiliation and strike down those who oppressed Him, He willingly laid down His life for us.

> He was oppressed, and he was afflicted, yet he opened not his mouth; like a lamb that is led to the slaughter, and like a sheep that before its shearers is silent, so he opened not his mouth. (Isa. 53:7)

> I gave My back to those who strike Me, And My cheeks to those who pluck out the beard; I did not cover My face from humiliation and spitting. (Isa. 50:6)

Let me recommend the following prayer written by Raphael Cardinal Merry del Val for a set of terms that gives us perspective into the humility of Christ, and the radical call of dying to self.

> O Jesus meek and humble of heart, hear me.
> From the desire of being esteemed,
> from the desire of being loved,
> from the desire of being extolled,
> from the desire of being honored,
> from the desire of being praised,
> from the desire of being preferred to others,
> from the desire of being consulted,
> from the desire of being approved,
> from the fear of being humiliated,
> from the fear of being despised,
> from the fear of suffering rebukes,
> from the fear of being falsely accused,
> from the fear of being forgotten,
> from the fear of being ridiculed,
> from the fear of being wronged,
> from the fear of being suspected,
> deliver me, O Jesus.
>
> That others may be loved more than I,
> that others may be esteemed more than I,
> that, in the opinion of the world,
> others may increase and I may decrease,
> that others may be chosen and I set aside,
> that others may be praised and I unnoticed,
> that others may be preferred before me in everything,
> that others become holier than I,
> provided that I may become as holy as I should.
> Jesus, grant me the grace to desire it.[3]

LESSON 6 EXAM

Use the exam sheet at the back of the course to complete your exam.

1. **What is pride rooted in?**
   A. Being a leader
   B. Anything that gives you value outside of Christ
   C. People who have lots of money
   D. The practice of bragging

2. **How do we "move up" in God's eyes?**
   A. By performing righteous deeds
   B. By humbling ourselves
   C. By fasting publicly
   D. By reading the Bible every day

3. **Humility comes from**
   A. our status in society.
   B. comparing ourselves and our position to others.
   C. our circumstances.
   D. a right standing before God.

4. **Favoritism is**
   A. evil because it forces others into a lower place.
   B. acceptable if the person deserves honor.
   C. not a good practice but it is not a sin.
   D. a good way to humble someone.

5. **When Job's friends visited him,**
   A. they succeeded in comforting him.
   B. they helped him find purpose in his suffering.
   C. they made him feel better.
   D. they provoked him to defensiveness.

6. **Why didn't Job find joy in his suffering?**
   A. Because he deserved more respect
   B. Because he had not humbled himself
   C. Because he covered himself
   D. Because he didn't listen to his friends

7. Isaiah 66:2 reveals that our attitude in approaching God should be

A. humble.
B. contrite.
C. trembling.
D. all of the above.

8. To gain humility, we must

A. get rid of all the sin in our lives.
B. remove any trace of joy from our lives.
C. empty ourselves.
D. practice physical self-harm.

9. What is God's response to the proud?

A. He is gracious and lenient.
B. He is near to those proud in heart.
C. He isn't pleased but He will receive them.
D. He is opposed to the proud.

10. Jesus demonstrated humility by

A. living among His creation as a man.
B. not retaliating against unjust accusations.
C. not striking back at those who harmed Him.
D. all of the above.

What Do You Say?

What aspect of Christ's humility is most striking to you at this time?

LESSON 7

Repentance

I had heard of you by the hearing of the ear, but now my eye sees you; therefore I despise myself, and repent in dust and ashes. (Job 42:5-6)

We live every day with a death sentence; every day we pick up the dying of Jesus. Every day we embrace weakness, accept suffering, and choose humility. There is one more step in this walk of dying: repentance, the final nail in the coffin, the critical step between dying and living. Without repentance there is no change of heart or mind. Without repentance you continue in the wrong direction. Without repentance you can't live by the Spirit.

Pride is the heartbeat of the flesh. Living by the unmerited favor of God's grace weakens the heartbeat of the flesh and silences the protests of our pride. To die to self, pride must be dealt a fatal blow. Weakness hurts it, suffering offends it, and humility suffocates it. Repentance finishes it off.

Feeling Sorry vs. Repentance

"Sorry"—a word that by itself says very little. "Oh, sorry!" we say, meaning "excuse me." We tell a child who has made another child cry, "Say you're sorry." "Sawwwy" he says, but what does he think that means? Does he think it is a magic word like "please"? Saying sorry could be the means of avoiding punishment, a loophole that gets you out of trouble. "I'm sorry," we say, but we don't mean it.

Without repentance you can't live by the Spirit.

If I feel sorry, does that mean I've repented? What am I usually sorry for? Sometimes I feel sorry for getting caught or for letting myself down or for disappointing others. I often feel sorry for making a mistake, for being less than perfect, for opening myself up for blame, criticism, and judgment. I feel sorry for myself when I make someone angry at me. I feel sorry for the consequences of my mistakes. Do any of these feelings mean I have repented?

The dictionary says that *repentance* is "sincere regret or remorse." I'm familiar with regret, familiar with reliving, over and over again, each of my regrets.

- Why didn't I learn faster?
- Why didn't I stop talking before I said those things?
- Why couldn't I do it right?
- Why did I get jealous?
- Why wasn't I strong enough to avoid depression?
- Why did I lose my temper?
- Why was I destructive to others and to my relationships?
- Why didn't I say "no"!

Regrets. First they torment, then they anger. I regret my failures because I want to think of myself as better than that, because I fear that others will think less of me.

My regret is always sincere. Does that mean I have repented?

The Biblical definition of repentance is very different from the dictionary definition. Biblical repentance is to change your mind and turn to the Lord. This definition was lost in the Latin translation, so that today, all we have is this idea of feeling sorry and regret. But regret and remorse have nothing to do with true repentance.

The first step of repentance is to *turn*. The problem is that we can sit in remorse and regret indefinitely, never turning around. What's worse, regret and remorse can be born of the flesh, born of self-love, self-hate, and self-centeredness. In fleshly regret we label our sin as "mistakes," and, given enough time, we work out our own justification for having "made a mistake." Fleshly regret and remorse dump us in a cesspool of guilt and shame where we wallow until the pain subsides and we feel strong enough to keep going. In this, we have not repented nor have we turned to God!

Put It Down and Turn Around

What if you just blew it—lost your temper, yelled at your kids, lied to your boss, looked at pornography, got jealous? Whatever it was, you blew it. What now? You might feel sorry because you've embarrassed yourself, or exposed yourself to the possibility that others will think less of you. You might alternate between convincing yourself that you aren't that bad, fretting about what others think, excusing your lapse of perfection, and beating yourself up for having failed to keep it together. Wasn't it just a few days ago that you said you would never do that again?

Often we retreat until the bad feeling passes, but we should turn to God and admit defeat. Like the prodigal son who comes to his senses, we should "drop the slop" and return, broken and humble, to the Father (see Luke 15:11-24). Retreating is easier than accepting defeat, but it doesn't produce a change of heart, doesn't change direction to face God. Our habit of retreating causes us to repeat the same sins over and over again.

To pick up your cross you'll have to put something else down.

- You'll have to put down your rebellion.
- You'll have to put down your sin.
- You'll have to put down your pride.
- You'll have to put down that thing you refuse to give up.
- You'll have to put down those other things you love.
- You'll have to put down your will.

To walk by the Spirit you'll have to *put it down and turn around.*

What Is True Repentance?

True repentance is turning around and standing before the One greater than you, who has the right to judge you, and saying, "Here I stand Lord, wretchedly out of reach, with no hope of crossing over to You. Here I stand in the stench of my filthy rags of sin. What an offensive mess I bring into Your presence! I have sinned against You, and You are right to call me out on it and have the right to punish me."

True repentance is ...

- seeing your sin as God sees it, without trying to justify it.
- acknowledging God's perfect justice and rightness in punishing your sin, abandoning all hope of being able to make things right, and throwing yourself on God's grace and mercy.
- recognizing that you cannot, in any way, recover from your sin.
- making your appeal based on who God is, not on anything that you have done.
- bending down in submission to accept the cross that identifies you with Christ.
- action

- dying to self.
- freedom from sin.
- the step that finally breaks the cycle of defeat—completing it instead of repeating it.

Do you need to change your mind about …

- the reward for doing good.
- the idea that you have rights.
- the view that weakness is bad.
- the pursuit of feeling good about yourself.
- the justice of God.
- the practice of elevating yourself.
- the fluctuation of self-worth.

The flesh will not offer itself up to die, will not surrender, will not release us to the Spirit's control. Living by the Spirit means a walk of dying to self. God has built the method of dying to self into our Christian lives by making us weak, bringing us suffering, and humbling us. We need to embrace weakness, accept suffering, and choose humility. But those, on their own, will not be enough. We must also take this most fatal step for the flesh, the step of repentance. Don't say, "Oh I need to repent," or "that was bad, I shouldn't do it again," and then walk away staying stuck in discouragement over your failings and forget to put it down and turn around.

The flesh will not offer itself up to die, will not release us to the Spirit's control.

Acknowledging your mistake, or poor choice, or even failure to yourself won't empower you to be different, to stop repeating your defeat. And while confession to others may make you feel better, you haven't humbled yourself before the One who is worthy.

It's easy to rely on self-correction and think we've repented, but nothing can replace the physical act of getting on your knees before God and confessing your sin. In His presence you see your sin through His eyes, and that is where you are when true repentance occurs.

This lesson is short because action, not explanation, is needed. Nothing can be said that will make you feel more ready to begin this walk of dying. Take the first step: put it down and turn around. Repent!

LESSON 7 EXAM

Use the exam sheet at the back of the course to complete your exam.

1. **What does the author mean by this statement: "We live every day with a death sentence"?**
   A. We are dead in our sins.
   B. We live in judgement.
   C. We are to pick up our cross and die to self everyday.
   D. We are not actually alive.

2. **Repentance means**
   A. to apologize.
   B. to feel sorry for my actions.
   C. to regret my choices.
   D. to change my mind about my sin and turn from it.

3. **Regret**
   A. kills the flesh.
   B. will keep you stuck in the flesh.
   C. means the same thing as repentance.
   D. resolves a person's guilt.

4. **Fleshly regret and remorse will**
   A. minimize our sin as mistakes.
   B. lead us to try harder the next time.
   C. keep us stuck in guilt and shame.
   D. all of the above.

5. **When we "blow it" by sinning, we should**
   A. retreat into isolation until the bad feelings pass and try again.
   B. try to fix the damage done to others' perception of us.
   C. turn to God in repentance.
   D. beat ourselves up until our hearts change.

6. **What does true repentance result in?**
   A. Dying to self
   B. Pity for oneself
   C. Correcting self
   D. Promoting self

7. **When dealing with the flesh, it is good to know that the flesh**
   A. will eventually die on its own.
   B. can live in peace alongside the Spirit.
   C. will offer itself up to die.
   D. none of the above.

8. **True repentance requires**
   A. feeling sorry for yourself.
   B. guilt.
   C. action.
   D. all of the above.

9. **True repentance occurs when**
   A. you feel bad about what you did.
   B. you see your sin through God's eyes.
   C. you have others scold you.
   D. you acknowledge your mistake.

10. **The four steps in dying to self are**
   A. meekness, regret, repentance, and truth.
   B. weakness, confession, suffering, and repentance.
   C. weakness, suffering, humility, and repentance.
   D. love, remorse, confession, and faith.

What Do You Say?

In your life, what makes you hesitate from repenting when you see an area of sin?

LESSON 8

Walking in Truth, Part 1

I have no greater joy than this, to hear of my children walking in the truth. (3 John 1:4)

Up to this point, we have sought to identify the flesh and how it works in our life, and we have examined in Scripture four tools God uses to help us put the flesh to death—weakness, suffering, humility, repentance. Now we will look at the role of the Holy Spirit in our lives, and learn why we must walk in complete dependence on the Spirit.

The Bible teaches us about a number of significant areas in this life of following Christ in which the Spirit's role is so indispensable that any fleshly input is detrimental. The three areas we will look at are *walking in truth*, *walking in love*, and *prayer*.

The Spirit of Truth

Jesus promised His followers that when He left them, the Father would send the Spirit to be the Helper who would teach them and guide them in truth.

> And I will ask the Father, and He will give you another Helper, that He may be with you forever; that is the Spirit of truth, whom the world cannot receive, because it does not behold Him or know Him, but you know Him because He abides with you, and will be in you. (John 14:16-17)

> But the Helper, the Holy Spirit, whom the Father will send in my name, He will teach you all things, and bring to your remembrance all that I said to you. (John 14:26)

> When the Helper comes, whom I will send to you from the Father, that is the Spirit of truth, who proceeds from the Father, He will testify about Me. (John 15:26)

> But when He, the Spirit of truth, comes, He will guide you into all the truth. (John 16:13a)

In a letter John wrote to the churches he said,

> By this we know that we abide in Him and He in us, because He has given us of His Spirit. And we have seen and testify that the Father has sent the Son to be the Savior of the world. Whoever confesses that Jesus is the Son of God, God abides in him, and he in God. (1 John 4:13-15)

> The one who believes in the Son of God has the testimony in himself; the one who does not believe God has made Him a liar, because he has not believed in the testimony that God has given concerning His Son. And the testimony is this, that God has given us eternal life, and this life is in His Son. (1 John 5:10-11)

It is a simple equation:

> He who has the Son has the life; he who does not have the Son of God does not have the life. These things I have written to you who believe in the name of the Son of God, so that you may know that you have eternal life. (1 John 5:12-13)

Have you agreed that Jesus Christ is God? Have you believed that He came to this world to be your Savior, to die for your sins? There is no witness without the Spirit; there is no Spirit without new life in Christ. If you believe in the Son, you have life and the Spirit is the witness within you to that life.

> It is the Spirit who testifies, because the Spirit is the truth. (1 John 5:6b)

> In Him, you also, after listening to the message of the truth, the gospel of salvation—having also believed, you

> were sealed in Him [Christ] with the Holy Spirit of promise, who is given as a pledge of our inheritance. (Eph. 1:13-14a)

The Spirit, always there, always sure, bears witness within me, reminding me of my position in God's family, of the love of the Father, of the truth, of the words of Christ, and of the mind of God.

How Do We Arrive at Truth?

> I have not written to you because you do not know the truth, but because you do know it, and because no lie is of the truth. (1 John 2:21)

What is truth? How do you arrive at the truth, and how do you know what truth you should believe? Is truth based on facts, is it measured by the mounds of evidence, is it found in consistency, is it discovered through the most convincing argument?

In the scientific world, a fact is a truth based on highest probability arrived at by testing. A scientific fact is never final; it can be changed or discarded if new evidence appears. So, fact does not make truth.

We are all prone to consider true whatever we *already* believe to be true, and to filter any further evidence as reliable if it supports our truth, or as unreliable if it doesn't. We are also prone to believe to be true that which we *want* to believe is true.

The reality of human nature, the flesh, is that we are not good at knowing or finding truth; we are not as consistent with truth as we like to think we are. We may say that we arrive at the truth through inquiry, proof, and logic, but we have consistently proven that we are irrational, that we are predisposed to believe certain things, and that we are easily intimidated into believing something, even without supporting evidence.

We like to think that we are rational beings, capable of thinking our way to truth. But then, our version of the truth makes total sense to us, and seems rational from our perspective. We think we have all the proof we need to be convinced of our truth, and can't understand why others don't see it.

Don't be deceived; you can't arrive at truth in the flesh. Revealing truth is the indispensable role of the Spirit.

Revealing truth is the indispensable role of the Spirit.

The Mind

Sometimes our thoughts run away with us. We find ourselves flattened by the things we think. They carry us away, bouncing us along against our will. Do you ever feel as if you are at the mercy of your mind, that it chooses to run off with your thoughts and you can do nothing to stop it?

Do you ever find that your thoughts have built walls around you, blocking out reality?

> For though we walk in the flesh [as in, we are in these bodies until we die or are taken up with Christ], we do not war according to the flesh, for the weapons of our warfare are not of the flesh, but divinely powerful for the destruction of fortresses. We are destroying speculations and every lofty thing raised up against the knowledge of God, and we are taking every thought captive to the obedience of Christ. (2 Cor. 10:3-5)

Fortresses, according to Strong's concordance, is not a common word in Greek, but is used here, figuratively, of false arguments which often serve as a refuge from reality.[1] Where are those fortresses that divine weapons can tear down? This war is being waged in our *mind* every waking moment and sometimes even in our sleep.

God's Word has much to say about the mind. For instance, "loving God with all your mind" (Deut. 6:5), and "the mind set on the flesh is death" (Rom. 8:6), and "set your mind on things above" (Col. 3:2). We are exhorted to "gird up our minds" (1 Peter 1:13), and to "renew our minds" (Rom. 12:2). And there are several different Greek words referring to the mind.

nous

The Greek word *nous* means "mind, reason, or intellect."[2] Not every occurrence of this word in the Bible is included here. I have specifically chosen ones that relate to our walk. You will find the form of the word in bold type.

> But I see a different law in the members of my body, waging war against the law of my **mind**, and making me a prisoner of the law of sin which is in my members. Wretched man that I am! Who will set me free from the body of this death? Thanks be to God through Jesus Christ our Lord! So then,

on the one hand I myself with my **mind** am serving the law of God, but on the other, with my flesh the law of sin. (Rom. 7:23-25)

For who has known the **mind** of the Lord or who became His counselor. (Rom. 11:34)

And do not be conformed to this world but be transformed by the renewing of your **mind**. (Rom. 12:2)

Now I exhort you, brethren, by the name of our Lord Jesus Christ, that you all agree and that there be no divisions among you, but that you be made complete in the same **mind** and in the same judgment. (1 Cor. 1:10)

For who has known the **mind** of the Lord, that he will instruct him? But we have the **mind** of Christ. (1 Cor. 2:16)

For if I pray in a tongue, my spirit prays, but my **mind** is unfruitful. What is the outcome then? I will pray with the Spirit and I will pray with the **mind** also; I will sing with the Spirit and I will sing with the **mind** also. In the church, I desire to speak five words with my **mind**, so that I may instruct others also, rather than ten thousand words in a tongue. (1 Cor. 14:14-15, 19)

So this I say, and affirm together with the Lord, that you walk no longer just as the Gentiles also walk, in the futility of their **mind**, being darkened in their understanding. (Eph. 4:17-18a)

In reference to your former manner of life, you lay aside the old self, which is being corrupted in accordance with the lusts of deceit, and that you be renewed in the spirit of your **mind**, and put on the new self, which in the likeness of God has been created in righteousness and holiness of the truth. (Eph. 4:22-24)

And the peace of God, which surpasses all **comprehension**, will guard your hearts and your mind in Christ Jesus. (Phil. 4:7)

> Let no one keep defrauding you of your prize by delighting in self-abasement and the worship of the angels, taking his stand on visions he has seen, inflated without cause by his fleshly **mind**, and not holding fast to the head, from whom the entire body, being supplied and held together by the joints and ligaments, grows with a growth which is from God. (Col. 2:18-19)

In summary, we are told that, though the Lord's mind is beyond our grasp, we have the mind of Christ! We serve the law of God with our minds and, in doing so, find freedom from sin. The fleshly mind does not hold fast to the mind of Christ, but leads us astray to fleshly things like visions, the worship of created beings, and pleasure in self-harm. Before Christ, our minds took us in useless directions, but our minds are transformed when we abandon the old lusts of the flesh and put on the new self, created in righteousness and truth.

LESSON 8 EXAM

Use the exam sheet at the back of the course to complete your exam.

1. **Jesus asked the Father to send another Helper to His followers. To whom was He referring?**
   A. The Christ
   B. The Pastor
   C. The Shepherd
   D. The Spirit of truth

2. **According to 1 John 5:10-11, those who do not agree with the Son of God are calling Him**
   A. God of all.
   B. mean.
   C. a liar.
   D. weak.

3. **Those who have agreed with God unto salvation are recipients of**
   A. new life.
   B. the Holy Spirit.
   C. eternal life.
   D. all of the above.

4. **What does the Spirit do for those who have believed in Jesus Christ?**
   A. Abides in them
   B. Seals them in Christ
   C. Both A and B
   D. Neither A and B

5. **In the scientific world, a fact is**
   A. the highest probability after testing.
   B. never final.
   C. absolute truth.
   D. both A and B.

6. **The fleshly mind will**
   A. lead us to the truth.
   B. lead us astray.
   C. lead us to wise decisions.
   D. lead us to Christ.

7. **How can we know what is truth?**
   A. Test to find the highest probability
   B. Through inquiry, proof, and logic
   C. The Spirit is truth and guides us into all truth
   D. None of the above

8. **According to 2 Corinthians 10:3-5, we do war with divinely powerful weapons. Where does that battle occur?**
   A. In the world
   B. In the church
   C. In the mind
   D. In the heart

9. **While Paul says the flesh is serving the law of sin, what does he indicate our mind should serve?**
   A. Ourselves
   B. Others
   C. God
   D. The Law of God

10. **What is glorious about the mind of a believer?**
   A. It will one day be eliminated.
   B. It serves God without fault.
   C. It is the mind of Christ.
   D. It can be controlled through careful routines.

What Do You Say?

What does it mean to you that believers have "the mind of Christ"?

____

____

____

____

LESSON 9

Walking in Truth, Part 2

In the last lesson, we explored one of the Greek words used for "mind" in the New Testament—*nous*. If you look back, you will see in Philippians 4:7 that *nous* is translated as "comprehension." That is not a typo; in that passage, another Greek word is used for "mind," which leads us to *noema*.

noema

This Greek word means "the mind, thought, purpose, or scheme." With the exception of Philippians 4:7, it is used exclusively in 2 Corinthians.

> If I have forgiven anything, I did it for your sakes in the presence of Christ, so that no advantage be taken of us by Satan, for we are not ignorant of his **schemes**. (2 Cor. 2:10b-11)

> But their **minds** were hardened; for until this very day at the reading of the old covenant the same veil remains unlifted, because it is removed in Christ. (2 Cor. 3:14)

> And even if our gospel is veiled, it is veiled to those who are perishing, in whose case the god of this world has blinded the **minds** of the unbelieving so that they might not see the light of the gospel of the glory of Christ, who is the image of God. (2 Cor. 4:3-4)

> We are taking every **thought** captive to the obedience of Christ. (2 Cor. 10:5b)

> I am afraid that as the serpent deceived Eve by his craftiness, your **minds** will be led astray from the simplicity and purity of devotion to Christ. (2 Cor. 11:3)

> And the peace of God, which surpasses all comprehension, will guard your hearts and your **minds** in Christ Jesus. (Phil. 4:7)

Here we see Satan's scheming mind, see him blinding the minds of unbelievers, and leading our minds astray. It also seems to reveal weak minds, hardened minds, vulnerable minds, and desperately needy minds.

Let's recap Paul's exhortation to the Philippians. Don't worry about anything, but pray about everything. Make your requests known to God. And God's peace, which is vastly beyond all your reasoning and intellect, will act as a guard, surrounding and protecting your heart and mind from attack.

phroneo

This Greek word means "to think, to have understanding, to observe, to have in mind." The list below includes most occurrences of *phroneo*.

> He [Jesus] rebuked Peter, and said, "Get behind me Satan; for you are not **setting your mind** on God's interests, but man's." (Mark 8:33)

> For those who are according to the flesh **set their minds** on the things of the flesh, but those who are according to the Spirit, the things of the Spirit. (Rom. 8:5)

> **Set your mind** on the things above not on the things that are on earth. (Col. 3:2)

> For through the grace given to me I say to everyone among you not to **think more highly** of himself than he ought to **think**; but to **think** so as to have sound judgment, as God has allotted to each a measure of faith. (Rom. 12:3)

> Be of the same **mind** toward one another; do not be haughty in **mind**, but associate with the lowly. Do not be wise in your own estimation. (Rom. 12:16)

> Now may the God who gives perseverance and encouragement grant you to be of the same **mind** with one another according to Christ Jesus. (Rom. 15:5)
>
> Make my joy complete by being of the same **mind**, maintaining the same love, united in spirit, **intent** on one purpose. (Phil. 2:2)
>
> Have this **attitude** in yourselves which was also in Christ Jesus. (Phil. 2:5)
>
> I urge Euodia and I urge Syntyche to **live in harmony** in the Lord. (Phil. 4:2)
>
> I press on toward the goal for the prize of the upward call of God in Christ Jesus. Let us therefore, as many as are perfect, have this **attitude**; and if in anything you have a different **attitude**, God will reveal that also to you; however, let us keep **living by** that same standard to which we have attained. Brethren, join in following my example, and observe those who walk according to the pattern you have in us. For many walk, of whom I often told you, and now tell you even weeping, that they are enemies of the cross of Christ, whose end is destruction, whose god is their appetite, and whose glory is in their shame, who **set their minds** on earthly things. (Phil. 3:14-19)

Walking with our mind set on the Spirit takes intention and effort.

Look at these two verses in Philippians again: "make my joy complete by being of the same **mind**, maintaining the same love, united in spirit, **intent** on one purpose." And "I urge Euodia and I urge Syntyche to **live in harmony** in the Lord." Unity in the body of Christ is achieved in the mind. Harmony is a way of thinking, and the biggest obstacle to unity is our self-consumed thoughts. The mind set on the Spirit is a team player. It doesn't seek its own glory, but looks out for the interests of others. If you are living in discord and division with your brothers and sisters in Christ, seeing them as enemies of yourself in

Walking with our mind set on the Spirit takes intention and effort.

opposition, functioning independently from your church, or tend to pull away rather than bond—you are not looking out for God's interests.

> Therefore I, [Paul,] prisoner of the Lord, implore [plead with] you to walk in a manner worthy of the calling with which you have been called, with all humility and gentleness, with patience, showing tolerance for one another in love, being diligent to preserve the unity of the Spirit in the bond of peace. (Eph. 4:1-3)

phronema

This is the Greek word for "thought, purpose, aspirations, or thought that results in behavior." It appears only four times, each of those in Romans 8.

> For the **mind** set on the flesh is death, but the **mind** set on the Spirit is life and peace, because the **mind** set on the flesh is hostile toward God. (Rom. 8:6-7a)

> And He who searches the hearts knows what the **mind** of the Spirit is, because He intercedes for the saints according to the will of God. (Rom. 8:27)

dianoia

This word represents the "mind, understanding, intellect, and disposition." It is the word for *mind* that we find in the most important commandment the Lord gave us.

> Love the Lord your God with all your heart, and with all your soul, and with all your **mind**. (Mark 12:30, NIV)

> Among them we too all formerly lived in the lusts of our flesh, indulging the desires of the flesh and of the **mind**, and were by nature children of wrath, even as the rest. (Eph. 2:3)

> Being darkened in their **understanding**, excluded from the life of God because of the ignorance that is in them, because of the hardness of their heart. (Eph. 4:18)

> Although you were formerly alienated and hostile in **mind**, engaged in evil deeds, yet He has now reconciled you in His

> fleshly body through death, in order to present you before Him holy and blameless and beyond reproach. (Col. 1:21)

> I will put My laws into their **minds**, and I will write them upon their hearts. (Heb. 8:10)

> I will put My laws upon their heart, and on their **mind** I will write them. (Heb. 10:16b)

> Therefore, prepare your **minds** for action, keep sober in spirit, fix your hope completely on the grace to be brought to you at the revelation of Jesus Christ. (1 Peter 1:13)

> And we know that the Son of God has come, and has given us **understanding**, so that we may know Him who is true; and we are in Him who is true, in His Son Jesus Christ. (1 John 5:20)

If God had not written on our wicked minds that which is true, we would be unable to love Him. We can't let our minds go to chaos; we must discipline them to always be on the alert, ready for battle.

logizomai

This Greek word can be interpreted a number of ways: reckon, consider, think, compute, or reason. *Logizomai* occurs about 20 times in the book of Romans; more than half the occurrences are in chapter 4 and translated "reckon." It shows up here in my list because of its use in Philippians 4:8.

> Finally, brethren, whatever is true, whatever is honorable, whatever is right, whatever is pure, whatever is lovely, whatever is of good repute, if there is any excellence and if anything worthy of praise, **dwell** on these things. (Phil. 4:8)

> [Love] does not **take into account** a wrong suffered. (1 Cor. 13:5c)

> Blessed is the man whose sin the Lord will not **take into account**. (Rom. 4:8)

> Even so, **consider** yourselves to be dead to sin, but alive to God in Christ Jesus. (Rom. 6:11)

> For I **consider** that the sufferings of this present time are not worthy to be compared with the glory that is to be revealed to us. (Rom. 8:18)

These verses focus on the determination and duration of the thoughts of our minds. We cannot always control what enters our minds, but we can determine what our minds dwell on. The thoughts we dwell on are those that we engage our mind to think on for an extended time in order to draw a conclusion.

We must not let our minds dwell on those things we are warned to avoid. Just as the Lord chooses not to dwell on our sin, so we should not let our minds dwell on the wrongs that others have committed against us. Just as He chooses not to keep a list of our offenses against Him to bring up over and over, so we should not keep an account of the offenses made against us. Don't let your mind keep that list of wrongs tucked away for those times you can pull it out to review and relive the hurt. Don't let your mind linger on lies, on lusts, on evil plots, on the ugly, or on another's bad reputation. Don't let your mind dwell on others' sin or on your own sin, but instead forgive and be forgiven.

To walk by the Spirit is to walk in truth, to choose truth over all other thoughts.

Do let your mind dwell on the truth. Do let your mind linger on the honorable, the right, the pure, the lovely, the good reputation, the excellent, and the praiseworthy. Do let your mind think about suffering, but only if in doing so, your sum totals up to be far inferior to the glory awaiting you in heaven; otherwise, don't let your mind go there.

Loving the Truth

To walk by the Spirit is to walk in truth, to choose truth over all other thoughts, to commit to think only on those things that are true. Dwelling on the uncertain events of the future is appealing, but it is not dwelling on truth. We are commanded not to worry about tomorrow, since today has enough troubles of its own. Yet we keep choosing to dwell on what might happen, on what others might think of us, or on what we can't change.

Worrying is not loving the truth. Making your feelings your source of truth, is not loving truth. Entertaining lies is not loving the truth. Blurring truth by claiming lies don't exist, is not loving the truth.

Living by the Spirit will mean an unwavering commitment to thinking and loving truth, and only in the Spirit can you do this!

LESSON 9 EXAM

Use the exam sheet at the back of the course to complete your exam.

1. Philippians 4:7 assures us God's peace will guard

A. our minds.
B. our walk.
C. our hearts.
D. Both A and C.

2. Which of the following are we not instructed to "set our mind" on in verses contained in this lesson?

A. Heavenly things
B. Things of the Spirit
C. God's interests
D. Earthly things

3. The mind set on the Spirit has an attitude of

A. unity, harmony, and humility.
B. superiority, individuality, and confidence.
C. inferiority, inadequacy and incompetence.
D. sweetness, silliness, and sorrow.

4. Walking with our minds set on the Spirit

A. happens without thinking.
B. is like walking in the park.
C. takes intention and effort.
D. will be easy.

5. The biggest obstacle to church unity is

A. building projects.
B. the world.
C. self-consumed thoughts.
D. false teaching.

6. **Before we were saved, our minds were**
   A. darkened to understanding God's life.
   B. hostile to God.
   C. used to indulge the flesh.
   D. All of the above.

7. **When it comes to our thinking,**
   A. we can choose what to dwell on.
   B. if it doesn't affect our behavior, it's okay.
   C. the Bible is silent on what to think about.
   D. We can control all that enters our mind.

8. **When dwelling on suffering, what fact should we also remember?**
   A. We only are loved by God when we suffer.
   B. Psychologically, suffering benefits our mind.
   C. Suffering is an illusion.
   D. The promise of the immense glory to come.

9. **According to Philippians 4:8, believers are responsible to let their minds dwell on certain things. Which of these things is on that list?**
   A. Uncertainty of future events
   B. A list of hurts against you
   C. Things about others that are not true
   D. Things that are worthy of praise

10. **What habits are the opposite of loving the truth?**
    A. Worrying
    B. Speculating
    C. Lying
    D. All of the above

What Do You Say?

What would it look like for you to "Love the LORD your God" with all your mind today?

____

____

____

____

LESSON 10

Walking in Love

If we live by the Spirit, let us also walk by the Spirit. Let us not become boastful, challenging one another, envying one another. (Gal. 5:25-26)

The Spirit and the flesh do not share the same road. If I'm not crucifying the flesh, I'm not walking in the Spirit. If I'm not crucifying the flesh, I am carrying out its desires, and its desires are selfish. The flesh wants to put *me* at the center, not others. But walking in the Spirit isn't for our own benefit!

The evidence of a walk of dying is in our *relationships*. Scripture shows us that God is intensely interested in how we relate to others in His family. As a member of this family, we are charged to love the other children.

> Whoever believes that Jesus is the Christ is born of God; and whoever loves the Father loves the child born of Him. (1 John 5:1)

Loving Like Jesus Commanded

Love is one need we all have in common. Every human being wants to be loved, but how much do we want to give love? We long to be loved, but equal to that desire is our capacity to hate.

Do you have a hard time accepting love from others because you don't feel you deserve it? Do you find it easier to accept love when you feel you have done something to earn it?

The evidence of a walk of dying is in our *relationships*.

Likewise, do you believe that some people don't deserve to be loved? Have you ever felt that you wasted your love on someone? Do people have limited opportunities to gain your love? We often think of love as a reward that we give back to people who show love to us.

Our idea of love comes with guidelines:

- Love should never be difficult.
- Love should bring out the best version of you.
- Love should make you feel good.
- Love should never hurt or make you cry.
- Love should let you be yourself.
- Love should make everything better.
- Love should come naturally and easily; you shouldn't have to work at it.

There are two inherent dangers with this concept of love. First, if real love is easy, then we will think that it wasn't difficult for God to love us. Second, if we expect love to be easy, we won't succeed in walking in the Spirit. We will turn back to flesh the moment love gets hard, and it *will* get hard.

We are called to a different type of love, and the call came from Jesus Himself. On the fateful night He was taken by soldiers to be tortured and crucified, Jesus told His disciples:

> A new commandment I give to you, that you love one another, even as I have loved you, that you also love one another. By this all men will know that you are my disciples, if you have love for one another. (John 13:34-35)

We can easily dismiss people we find hard to love, but Jesus doesn't. Think about the disciples. Did any of them deserve to be loved? One friend has sold Jesus' trust and is ready to betray Him; another will deny ever knowing Him. His closest friends won't be able to stay awake to pray for Him and support Him in His pain. And during this time, all they can do is argue about who will be the greatest.

Jesus loved even when it was painful. And we are called to this same love.

Do you think it was easy for Him to love them? No. Despite this, knowing they will abandon Him, He says to them, "You are those who have stood by Me in My trials" (Luke 22:28). Jesus loved even when it was painful, when it hurt. And we are called to this same love.

To love in the Spirit is to love even the most difficult people you will ever meet, without merit and without limit.

Loving in the Flesh or the Spirit?

Are you trying to love someone in the flesh? It won't work, because the flesh only knows selfish love. The flesh corrupts and destroys love. Think about your relationships in your home, in your church, in your life, and compare them with this list. What corrupting influence has the flesh had in your relationships?

Of others, are you ever . . .

- suspicious
- jealous
- critical
- harsh
- resentful
- dismissive
- intolerant
- indifferent

To others, do you ever respond with . . .

- impatience
- insecurity
- negativity
- competition
- self-pity
- bragging
- gossip
- revenge
- partiality
- ultra-sensitivity
- blame

Also consider these questions to determine if you are loving in the Spirit:

- Whom can you not stand to be around?
- Whom do you make fun of with your friends?
- Who gives you pleasure when you see them fail?
- Who has a weakness that you recall to mind in order to feel superior?
- Whom are you cutting off because they don't recognize your abilities or value you enough?
- Who are you trying to impress?
- Who has something you wish you had?
- Whom do you avoid because they aren't popular?
- Who has hurt you deeply, and seems impossible to forgive?
- Who owes you?
- Who tries your patience?
- Whom do you frequently get angry with and yell at?

- Whom do you criticize?
- Whom do you complain about?
- Who has let you down?
- Whom do you never pray for?
- Whom have you cut off from your concern?
- Whom do you want to be better than?
- Whom do you tell yourself you could love if only they were more loving to you first?

Do you wish that people in your church were more loving? Do you complain about their lack of love? Maybe it hasn't occurred to you that you are one of those people who aren't loving? The Lord has placed you with these people to teach you to walk in the Spirit.

Jesus commanded us to love others, not to be loved.

Calvary Love

When Jesus told us who to love, he said to love each other. But we are not just called to love our friends; He also said to love our enemies.

Sometimes I feel that I will never "graduate" from this commandment. If I had my choice, I would pretty much do anything other than love the unlovable, or to love someone who doesn't love me back.

If we withhold love (even a little bit), or if we love based on whether we believe the person deserves it, then we are not loving as Christ has loved us. As Amy Carmichael said in her book *IF*, we know nothing of the love Christ showed us on Calvary.

We are not just called to love our friends; Jesus also said to love our enemies.

In the introduction to her book, Amy says that one evening another believer came to her with a problem involving a younger sister in Christ who had lost the way of love. Amy stayed awake all night, wondering if she had failed this sister somehow, wondering what she truly knew of "Calvary love." And then, one by one, the "ifs" came to her as if, she says, "spoken aloud in the inward ear." Here are a few of those "ifs."

"I know nothing of Calvary love …

- if I hold on to choices of any kind, just because they are my choice;
- if I give any room to my private likes and dislikes;
- if my thoughts revolve around myself;

- if I cannot in honest happiness take the second place (or the twentieth);
- if I cannot take the first without making a fuss about my unworthiness;
- if I do not give a friend 'the benefit of the doubt,' but put the worst construction instead of the best on what is said or done;
- if I take offense easily;
- if I am content to continue in a cool unfriendliness, though friendship be possible;
- if a sudden jar can cause me to speak an impatient, unloving word;
- if I feel bitterly towards those who condemn me, as it seems to me unjustly, forgetting that if they knew me as I know myself, they would condemn me much more;
- if monotony tries me and I cannot stand drudgery …
- if something I'm asked to do for another feels burdensome; and yielding to an inward unwillingness, I avoid doing it;
- if the praise of men elates me and his blame depresses me;
- if I cannot rest under misunderstanding without defending myself;
- if I love to be loved more than to love;

Then I know nothing of Calvary Love."[1]

Walking in Love

The body of Christ is where we learn to love others with Christlike love. There are a number of passages in Scripture that help us know what this love looks like. Many of them are straightforward, and some literally give us lists of how we should be demonstrating this love. So the challenge is really not a lack of information about what this love looks like. It's whether we will take seriously the type of love that is described in these passages.

> But **speaking the truth in love**, we are to grow up in all aspects into Him, who is the head, even Christ, from whom the whole body, being fitted and held together by that which every joint supplies, according to the proper working of each individual part, causes the growth of the body **for the building up of itself in love**. (Eph. 4:15-16)

> Above all, **keep fervent in your love for one another**, because **love covers a multitude of sins**. Be hospitable to one another without complaint. (1 Peter 4:8-9)
>
> **Let love be without hypocrisy.** Abhor what is evil; cling to what is good. **Be devoted to one another in brotherly love**; give preference to one another in honor. (Rom. 12:9-10)
>
> If I speak in the tongues of men or of angels, **but do not have love,** I am only a resounding gong or a clanging cymbal. If I have the gift of prophecy and can fathom all mysteries and all knowledge, and if I have a faith that can move mountains, **but do not have love, I am nothing.** If I give all I possess to the poor and give over my body to hardship that I may boast, but **do not have love,** I gain nothing.
>
> **Love is patient, love is kind. It does not envy, it does not boast, it is not proud. It does not dishonor others, it is not self-seeking, it is not easily angered, it keeps no record of wrongs. Love does not delight in evil but rejoices with the truth. It always protects, always trusts, always hopes, always perseveres. Love never fails.** (1 Cor. 13:1-8a)

When we think about walking in the Spirit, are we prepared for this kind of dying, for walking in this kind of love? If you think that you can't love that way, Jesus would answer, of course you can't: "Apart from Me you can do nothing" (John 15:5c).

Jesus called (commanded!) us to love others like He loved us—and gave us His Spirit to enable us to walk in that love.

LESSON 10 EXAM

Use the exam sheet at the back of the course to complete your exam.

1. **Equal to our desire to be loved is our capacity to**
   A. pray.
   B. hate.
   C. sing.
   D. walk.

2. **Real love is**
   A. hard.
   B. easy.
   C. natural.
   D. never painful.

3. **In John 13:34-35, Jesus gives us**
   A. His preference for those we should love.
   B. a defense of His choice of disciples.
   C. a new commandment to love one another.
   D. the reason He was betrayed.

4. **According to the same verses, how will the world know that you are a disciple of Christ?**
   A. By your prayers
   B. By the clothes you wear
   C. By how you love your brothers and sisters in Christ
   D. None of the above

5. **Jesus' example to us of loving one another included**
   A. picking the right friends.
   B. not dismissing difficult people.
   C. doing what was most convenient for Him.
   D. a time limit.

6. What is the only kind of love the flesh knows?
- A. Selfish love
- B. Romantic love
- C. Sacrificial love
- D. Unconditional love

7. Jesus commanded us to
- A. be loved.
- B. love others.
- C. both A and B.
- D. none of the above.

8. When you meet an enemy, Jesus would have you
- A. get revenge.
- B. ignore them.
- C. give them what they deserve.
- D. love them.

9. If you are loving others based on whether you think they deserve it,
- A. you are not loving as Christ has loved you.
- B. you can be sure you are pleasing God.
- C. you know Calvary love.
- D. none of the above.

10. In 1 Peter 4:8-9, we are told to
- A. crucify the flesh.
- B. be fervent in our love for one another
- C. show hospitality to one another
- D. both B and C.

What Do You Say?

Who is someone in your life you could, by the Spirit, practice showing "Calvary love" to?

LESSON 11 Jan. 28th, 2022

Walking in Prayer

Abba, Father, all things are possible for you. Remove this cup from me. Yet not what I will, but what you will. (Mark 14:36)

As we continue to learn how we are to walk in the Spirit, we come to the last area in our life that we will look at together—*prayer*. The Bible reveals to us that prayer and the Spirit go hand in hand.

Praying in the Flesh or the Spirit?

Ephesians 6:18 tells us to "pray at all times in the Spirit." Can we infer from this that it is possible to pray in the flesh? I believe we can. Jesus warned against praying like the Pharisees or Gentiles:

> And when you pray, you are not to be like the hypocrites; for they love to stand and pray in the synagogues and on the street corners so that they may be seen by men. Truly I say to you, they have their reward in full. But you, when you pray, go into your inner room, close your door and pray to your Father who is in secret, and your Father who sees what is done in secret will reward you. And when you are praying, do not use meaningless repetition as the Gentiles do, for they suppose that they will be heard for their many words. So do not be like them; for your Father knows what you need, before you ask Him. (Matt. 6:5-8)

When I pray, I do a lot of thinking. I think about what I'm going to say, about what others will think of what I say. I think about how long that person is praying, about how I wish I sounded as worshipful as someone else does. I think about what I will do after the prayer time is over, about what I want to say to the person next to me, or about my next task.

If I'm being particularly fleshly, I'll critique what others are saying, thinking about the shallowness of their prayer requests, and judging them for the mess they make of their lives. I'll wait for my requests to be prayed for, comparing whether sufficient time was given for my concerns and my needs, wondering why people don't care about me or think about me as much as they do another person.

That's what praying in the flesh looks like for me. This lesson focuses on prayer and what you can expect the Spirit to do, and the flesh to hinder.

Prayer and God's Will

You know how it is when someone is talking *at* you, not *with* you? Prayer ought to be a two-way communication, but it often looks like us talking at God. How much do we listen to God? Do we expect Him to talk to us?

When you pray, do you come to God with a closed mind, unwilling to change your thoughts? Are you interested in what God thinks, in what's on His mind? Maybe you don't want to know; maybe you don't want to change your plans.

What should be our primary goal in prayer? Is prayer for the purpose of communicating to God what's on our minds or listening to learn what's on His? Which is more important—that He knows our will, or that we know His? Doesn't He already know what we are thinking, even the motives of our heart, far better than we do?

God has made it possible for us to know His will, and listening to Him to understand His will ought to be the primary focus of our prayer life.

> Just as it is written, "things which eye has not seen and ear has not heard, and which have not entered the heart of man, all that God has prepared for those who love Him." For to us God revealed them through the Spirit; for the Spirit searches all things, even the depths of God. For who among men knows the thoughts of a man except the spirit of the man, which is in him? Even so the thoughts of God no one knows except the Spirit of God. Now we have received, not the spirit of the world, but the Spirit who is from God, so that we may know the things freely given to us by God, which things we also speak, not in words taught by human wisdom, but in those taught by the Spirit, combining spiritual thoughts with spiritual words. (1 Cor. 2:9-13)

> In the same way the Spirit also helps our weakness; for we do not know how to pray as we should, but the Spirit Himself intercedes for us with groanings too deep for words; and He who searches the hearts knows what the mind of the Spirit is, because He intercedes for the saints according to the will of God. (Rom. 8:26-27)

We cannot know one tiny smidgen of God's will, whether through His inspired written Word or through prayer, without the Spirit. So, whose mind or thoughts are you expressing when you pray? Maybe we should start praying by admitting our incapacity to know how or what to pray.

The Holy Spirit knows the mind of God. The Holy Spirit knows what God already has planned for us. When we learn to wait on Him in prayer, to want God's will first, the Holy Spirit will show us what to ask for. And we can be certain that the Spirit of truth will not lead in opposition to the Word of truth. The only way to pray according to the will of God is to pray in the Spirit.

The only way to pray according to the will of God is to pray in the Spirit.

> No prophecy was ever made by an act of human will, but men moved by the Holy Spirit spoke from God. (2 Pet. 1:21)

The same should be said about prayer: that no request has its origin in my will, but has come from God through the Holy Spirit.

Praying with Perseverance

Paul wrote to the church in Ephesus,

> With all prayer and petition pray at all times in the Spirit, and with this in view, be on the alert [be watchful, not asleep, vigilant, no time off, staying awake], with all perseverance [with all persistence, tenacity, steadfastness], and petition for all the saints. (Eph. 6:18)

To walk in the Spirit is to pray in the Spirit, and to pray in the Spirit is to pray with perseverance. So how can we gain perseverance in prayer? Stubbornness may help for a while, but stubbornness is just the flesh imitating perseverance. There is only one way to gain perseverance in prayer: through the Spirit. The flesh cannot produce alertness and tenacity in prayer.

According to Ephesians 6, prayer in the Spirit is always alert and watchful, ready to swing into action, ready to pray at a moment's notice, ready to keep praying. Are we including this aspect of watchfulness, of sensitivity to the Spirit's prompting, as part of our prayer life?

If there was ever a time that Jesus needed prayer it was that night in the garden before He was arrested. His agony was so deep that He asked His three closest disciples to watch and pray while He went off to pray by Himself. Returning to where He had left them, He found them sleeping.

> "Could you not watch one hour?" he said. "Keep watching and praying that you may not come into temptation; the spirit indeed is willing, but the flesh is weak." (Mark 14:37b-38)

Jesus went away by Himself a second time and returned to find them sleeping again "for their eyes were heavy" (Matt. 26:43). I can relate. I'm no different from Peter, James, and John. When it comes to praying, I'm weak, not a warrior.

Prayer in the Spirit is always alert and watchful.

The One who created our physical bodies to need sleep tells us to "stay awake." How are we to accomplish this? Does He mean that we are never to sleep? That's impossible! But staying awake for an hour is not impossible. I do it all the time, unless, of course, I'm praying, or reading the Bible. An all-night prayer vigil sounds excruciatingly painful, yet how easy it is for me to stay up all night reading a good book, or watching movies, or doing something else I really want to do. The flesh doesn't find it impossible to stay awake when what we want to do excites or appeals to us.

Stay Awake!

The physical weakness of the flesh in prayer is distractedness, sleepiness, or dullness. The emotional weakness of the flesh is growing weary and giving up when our prayers are not answered immediately.

> And he [Jesus] was telling them a parable to show that at all times they ought to pray and not lose heart. (Luke 18:1)

There was a judge in a certain city who didn't fear God or respect people. Now in that same city was a widow who kept coming to this judge, relentlessly asking for justice. Finally, the judge gave in, not because he feared God or respected people, but because she pestered him to no end.

The Lord wants us to see how the unjust judge gave in to persistence. That parable should cause us to ask ourselves, "Won't God also come to the aid of those who cry to him night and day? Will he be slow about it?"

> I tell you that he will give them justice quickly. (Luke 18:8a)

Then He asks this question:

> But when the Son of Man comes will he find faithfulness on earth? (Luke 18:8b)

Why does Jesus close the parable with this?

The purpose of the parable is stated at the beginning: to teach us to always pray without growing weary. Why is He concerned with whether He will find us faithful when He returns? What does He want to find us faithful in doing? Is there a relationship between prayer and end times?

About those last days Jesus warns,

> Be on guard, so that your hearts will not be weighted down with dissipation and drunkenness and the worries of life, and that day will not come on you suddenly like a trap; for it will come upon all those who dwell on the face of all the earth. But keep on the alert at all times, praying that you may have strength to escape all these things that are about to take place, and to stand before the Son of Man. (Luke 21:34-36)

He has just told them, as recorded earlier in this chapter, of the end of time, of how there will be terrifying signs from heaven, and they will be persecuted and betrayed even by family members. They will be hated by all because of Jesus, but if they endure they will be saved. When they see the Son of Man coming in a cloud with power and glory, they will know that the kingdom of God is near.

A parallel description of this teaching records Jesus saying,

> But concerning that day or that hour, no one knows, not even the angels in heaven, nor the Son, but only the Father. Be on guard, keep awake. For you do not know when the time will come. It is like a man going on a journey, when he leaves home and puts his servants in charge, each with his work, and commands the doorkeeper to stay

> awake. Therefore stay awake—for you do not know when the master of the house will come, in the evening, or at midnight, or when the rooster crows, or in the morning—lest he come suddenly and find you asleep. And what I say to you I say to all: Stay awake. (Mark 13:32-36, ESV)

What do praying and the coming of the Son of Man have in common? They both require watching, being alert, staying awake, and praying with faithfulness. Watch and pray until the Lord returns. Don't be caught sleeping.

> On your walls, O Jerusalem, I have set watchmen; all the day and all the night they shall never be silent. You who put the Lord in remembrance, take no rest, and give him no rest until he establishes Jerusalem and makes it a praise in the earth. (Isa. 62:6-7, ESV)

Our prayers must also be watchful, anticipating the Lord's return. We pray so that we can resist temptation. We pray so that we remain ready and alert. We pray to show that we are vigilant. We pray at all times because we don't know when His return will be.

Faithfulness is a fruit of the Spirit, so to be faithful in prayer, we must pray in the Spirit. In the flesh, we cannot hope to know how or what to pray; we cannot hope to stay awake or be tenacious enough to pray.

To be faithful in prayer, we must pray in the Spirit.

I offered to pray for someone once saying, "It's the least I can do." As soon as I uttered those words I realized how upside down my view of prayer was. My friend's story was heart-wrenching, and there was nothing I could do to help. So out of my own inadequacy I offered the only thing I could. Sadly, I viewed that as the least.

On the contrary, prayer is the *most* we can do. Walk in prayer!

> Devote yourselves to prayer, keeping alert in it with an attitude of thanksgiving. (Col. 4:2)

> Rejoice in hope, be patient in tribulation, be constant in prayer. (Rom. 12:12, ESV)

LESSON 11 EXAM

Use the exam sheet at the back of the course to complete your exam.

1. **What is an example of praying in the flesh?**
   - A. Judging how other people pray
   - B. Wondering why you weren't prayed for more
   - C. Praying with big words for attention
   - D. All of the above.

2. **What is the primary goal of prayer as described in this lesson?**
   - A. To tell God what you want
   - B. To thank God for things
   - C. To listen and understand God's will
   - D. None of the above

3. **The most important guidance in knowing God's will is**
   - A. the advice of the Pastor.
   - B. the role of the Spirit.
   - C. a book about discovering God's will.
   - D. hearing it in a dream.

4. **The Spirit of truth will ___________ lead us in opposition to the Word of truth.**
   - A. Never
   - B. Always
   - C. Sometimes
   - D. Possibly

5. **To pray in the Spirit is to pray**
   - A. with perseverance.
   - B. whenever you feel like it.
   - C. visibly so people can see you.
   - D. the same prayer every day.

6. **The flesh __________ produce alertness in prayer.**
   A. may
   B. cannot
   C. is willing to
   D. none of the above

7. **How is your physical and emotional weakness in prayer revealed?**
   A. By sleepiness
   B. By distractedness
   C. By growing weary
   D. All of the above

8. **When Jesus returns, what does He want to find you faithfully doing?**
   A. Living without any sin
   B. Watching with alertness
   C. Praying in the Spirit
   D. Both B and C

9. **In Mark 13:32-36, Jesus challenged His disciples to**
   A. move quickly.
   B. stand firm.
   C. stay awake.
   D. go fishing.

10. **The *most* (though not the only thing) that you can do for someone is**
   A. smile.
   B. give.
   C. pray.
   D. cook.

What Do You Say?

How does the Bible link prayer and the last days?

Prayerfully.

LESSON 12

Finding Life in Christ

It was for freedom that Christ set us free; therefore keep standing firm and do not be subject again to a yoke of slavery. (Gal. 5:1)

This has been a challenging study. It's a difficult and painful topic—but an important one. Let's take a moment to recall the concepts we've looked at together. First of all, remember that the flesh is out to get you, to drag you back into slavery and sin. It seeks to deceive you with deadly desire. The answer to the flesh's power is to respond to Christ's call to deny yourself, take up your cross daily, and follow Him (Luke 9:23). This is your *walk of dying.*

A walk of dying is the moment by moment choice to die to self.

A walk of dying is the moment by moment choice to die to self, to step with the Lord into the circumstances He designs—circumstances that make us feel weak, take us through suffering, pierce our pride, and lead us to humble repentance. A walk of dying means living a life of power in the Spirit—power to know the Truth, power to love as Christ loved, and the power to pray in His will.

In God's paradigm, only the dead can live, only the dead are free to walk by the Spirit. And experience freedom in finding life in Christ.

But how do you know where you are at in your walk? Let's take one more look at Galatians 5.

Life in the Body of Christ

Galatians 5 is a powerful mirror for us to find out how we are doing in this "flesh vs. Spirit" battle. In verses 13-15, it shows us that a good indicator is what we looked at in Lesson 10—*love.*

Paul says,

> For you were called to freedom, brethren; only do not turn your freedom into an opportunity for the flesh, but through love serve one another. For the whole Law is fulfilled in one word, in the statement, "You shall love your neighbor as yourself." But if you bite and devour one another, take care that you are not consumed by one another.

God has placed us in the Body of Christ, the church. It is one body with many parts. Sadly, it is in the church where we turn on our other parts with more viciousness than one might find in the world among those who have nothing of the Spirit. We often compete for position, to be the most spiritual, the most right, the most important. We fight for position like the disciples did in Luke 9:46.

What was it that the apostle Paul said about the mind of Christ? "Do nothing from selfish ambition or conceit; but in humility count others more significant than yourselves" (Phil. 2:3). Jesus, the very form of God, did not count His equality with God a thing to grasp, but emptied Himself, taking the form of a human, becoming a bondservant, obediently walking to death on the cross.

The living process was never meant to be done apart from the body of Christ, the church.

You must choose the cross every day in order to die to self. You must choose the cross every day, not for your own benefit but for the good of others. Isn't that why Christ took up His cross? He died so you could live.

Let's face it, church is hard. Living and working with people with whom we don't get along, people who seem to take pleasure in ruffling our feathers, people who bother and irritate us, who gossip about us, who hurt our feelings. Church is where we find it so easy to judge, to spread gossip, and to pick sides. We naturally tend towards an "us and them" mentality. It would be so much easier to "do church" at home, alone. It would be so much easier to be spiritual if we didn't have to work with others.

But the living process was never meant to be done apart from the body of Christ. The church is where we practice the dying process; if we are selfish and do not die to what we want, we won't stick around. Walking in the Spirit, or "Spirit-controlled walking," is the only way to truly live in the body of Christ.

Keep Dying to the Flesh

Paul continues on in Galatians 5, identifying the "works" or "deeds" of the flesh that we should be on watch for in our lives. This is what we looked at in Lesson 2; in order to kill the flesh in our lives, we must expose it.

> Now the deeds of the flesh are evident, which are: immorality, impurity, sensuality, idolatry, sorcery, enmities, strife, jealousy, outbursts of anger, disputes, dissensions, factions, envying, drunkenness, carousing, and things like these... Now those who belong to Christ Jesus have crucified the flesh with its passions and desires. (Gal. 5:19-21a, 24)

Take a moment to reflect. What thoughts are consuming you right now?

- What are you anxious about? What are you worried about? Are you preoccupied with what others think about you? Are you caught up in comparing yourself with others?
- Are your thoughts revolving around a hurt? Do you think about getting back at the ones who've hurt you? Do you review your lists of ways in which they hurt you? Do you wish pain on someone?
- What about sex? Are your thoughts on pornography? Do you have sexual fantasies that dominate your thinking? Do you entertain thoughts of sexual satisfaction outside of marriage?
- Do you think of yourself as better than others? Dream about wonderful things said about you? Or do your thoughts go in the opposite direction, overwhelming worthlessness?
- Do you think about juicy gossip? Are your thoughts often angry? Do you hate anyone? Is your mind filled with thoughts of rage?
- Do you dwell on unhappy thoughts? Do you wish your life was different? Is your mind filled with complaining?

These thoughts are a good indicator of your flesh weakness or weaknesses. Behind them is what gives you value, and behind that is your pride.

I expect that sometime during this course you've been actively dying to self, actively crucifying the flesh.

Those victories have been, and still are, very critical to the process. They are not for nothing as you might be tempted to think, because perhaps you find yourself failing to be strong—again.

Maybe you've slipped back where you didn't want to go, and now you're stepping in the familiar "muck" (sin), thinking there is no hope for change in your life. Don't let the flesh condemn you. Look at your feet. Yes, you are back in the muck but it's different this time. Before you would have been in up to your armpits—now you are only standing in it and as a result you've got a much better perspective on things. The Spirit has brought clarity much sooner than before. Be encouraged! This is progress!

Remember dying is what brings living. Weakness isn't discouraging, weakness is power!

Stop! Turn around! Pray! Ask the Lord to show you what He has intended to reveal. He has something for you to learn.

Ask and be still. And when you see your pride, repent.

If you're still bothered, dismayed, discouraged, angry, hurt, confused—go back and ask again. You didn't see your pride. It's there! And when you call it out, Jesus will calm the storm.

This is the dying process. Welcome it into your life.

Walk by the Spirit

Continuing in Galatians, we come once again to the fruit of the Spirit.

> But the fruit of the Spirit is love, joy, peace, patience, kindness, goodness, faithfulness, gentleness, self-control; against such things there is no law. Now those who belong to Christ Jesus have crucified the flesh with its passions and desires. If we live by the Spirit, let us also walk by the Spirit. (Gal. 5:22-25)

As we learned in Lesson 2, the fruit of the Spirit is not something you can manufacture on your own. It is the fruit, or evidence, of the Spirit at work in you. It was the power of the Spirit that raised us up to new life in Christ, and we should continue to walk by the Spirit's power and guidance.

- Are you showing pure, selfless *love* to those around you?
- Can others see *joy* in you as you go about your daily life?
- Do you experience *peace* in the midst of trials or hardships?
- Do you demonstrate *patience* in all circumstances?
- Are your interactions with others, believers and unbelievers, full of *kindness*?
- Could the things you do for others be viewed as acts of *goodness*?

- Is your life characterized by consistency and *faithfulness*?
- Do your words and actions exhibit quiet *gentleness*?
- Are you living a lifestyle that is seen to be under *self-control*?

So how can you live this way? How can you live a life that produces this type of fruit? Remember that you *can't* do it. We must not forget that, otherwise we will try to create this lifestyle on our own. Trying to do this on our own leads to moralistic or self-righteous living that is guided by our fleshly mindset, as opposed to the freedom of life in Christ that is guided by the Spirit. Remember what Paul said: "The mind governed by the flesh is death, but the mind governed by the Spirit is life and peace" (Rom. 8:6).

So approach your Christian life with the humility that you are too weak to accomplish this on your own. Surrender everything to God. Pray each day that the Spirit would be at work in you to crucify your flesh, its passion and desires, and enable you to daily walk by *His* power. When you are reading God's Word, ask that the Spirit would use it to expose your flesh, and to teach you how to walk by the Spirit. If you "draw near to God … He will draw near to you" (James 4:8a).

When you surrender your life and walk by the Spirit, you will begin to discover *true freedom*.

When you surrender your life and walk by the Spirit, you will begin to discover *true freedom*. Freedom from self, freedom from temptation, freedom from past sin. Will it be perfect? No. Not until we are with Christ will we be able to fully shed this body of sin and death. But the Scriptures are clear: "Where the Spirit of the Lord is, there is freedom" (2 Cor. 3:17b).

Finding Life in Christ

In conclusion, this process we've been examining—dying to flesh in order to walk by the Spirit—is all about *Christ*. It's so we can become like Jesus in His life, His death, and His resurrection.

In His *life*, Christ was filled with the Spirit to do what His Father called Him to do (Luke 3:21-23; 4:1, 14-21). The same Spirit lives in us in order to empower us to know Christ and be like Him, and to do what God calls us to do.

> For this reason I bow my knees before the Father, from whom every family in heaven and on earth derives its

> name, that He would grant you, according to the riches of His glory, to **be strengthened with power through His Spirit** in the inner man, so **that Christ may dwell in your hearts** through faith; and that you, being rooted and grounded in love, may be able to comprehend with all the saints what is the breadth and length and height and depth, and **to know the love of Christ** which surpasses knowledge, that you may be filled up to all the fullness of God. (Eph. 3:14-19)

In His *death*, Christ humbled Himself and, instead of choosing His own desires, was obedient to the point of death on a cross (Luke 22:42; Phil. 2:8). We are called to this same death—to humbly deny ourselves, and obediently take up our cross daily.

> **Always carrying about in the body the dying of Jesus**, so that the life of Jesus also may be manifested in our body. For we who live are constantly being delivered over to death for Jesus' sake, so that the life of Jesus also may be manifested in our mortal flesh. (2 Cor. 4:10-11)

In His *resurrection*, Jesus was raised from death to new life, achieving victory over sin and death. We live in this same victory, having been raised to new life—His life—in order that we might daily walk in it.

> Therefore we have been buried with Him through baptism into death, so that **as Christ was raised from the dead** through the glory of the Father, so **we too might walk in newness of life.** For if we have become united with Him in the likeness of His death, certainly we shall also be in the likeness of His resurrection. (Rom. 6:4-6)

So the call to *die to self and walk by the Spirit* is not just to help you be a better person, a moral person. It is so that you may find life in Christ (Col. 3:4). So that you can walk in the freedom of Christ (Gal. 5:1). So that you may "know him [Christ] and the power of his resurrection, and may share his sufferings, becoming like him in his death, that by any means possible [you] may attain the resurrection from the dead" (Phil. 3:10-11, ESV). It's all about Christ!

As you seek to crucify your flesh, relying on the Spirit in your daily walk, fix your eyes on Christ:

> If then you have been raised with Christ, seek the things that are above, where Christ is, seated at the right hand of God. Set your minds on things that are above, not on things that are on earth. For you have died, and your life is hidden with Christ in God. When Christ who is your life appears, then you also will appear with him in glory. (Col. 3:1-4)

One day, our battle with the flesh will be over. When Christ returns, we will put off this body of death and experience life and victory in the fullest. What a day of joy and peace that will be. Until then:

> Die to self.
> Walk by the Spirit.
> Find life in Christ.

LESSON 12 EXAM

Use the exam sheet at the back of the course to complete your exam.

1. **The answer to the flesh's power is**
   A. a walk of helping others.
   B. a walk of learning.
   C. a walk of dying.
   D. a walk of trying.

2. **Who is the ultimate example of humility?**
   A. Abraham
   B. Paul
   C. Peter
   D. Jesus Christ

3. **Life in the body of Christ, the church, is**
   A. always an easy and joyful experience.
   B. unrelated to the believer's process of dying to self.
   C. unnecessary.
   D. where believers practice the process of dying to self.

4. **Which of the following are NOT examples of fleshly thoughts?**
   A. Overwhelming worthlessness
   B. Revenge
   C. Sex with your spouse
   D. Complaining

5. **Weakness is**
   A. discouraging.
   B. proof of the flesh.
   C. to be avoided.
   D. power.

6. **One aspect of producing the fruit of the Spirit we can't forget is that**
   A. we can't produce it ourselves.
   B. we don't have to if circumstances are difficult.
   C. it depends primarily on how much you know of the Bible.
   D. God helps those who help themselves.

7. **Walking by the Spirit includes**
   A. being taught by the Spirit through God's Word.
   B. prayer.
   C. surrendering your life.
   D. all of the above.

8. **We should become like Christ in**
   A. His life.
   B. His death.
   C. His resurrection.
   D. All of the above.

9. **Walking by the Spirit is so**
   A. the world can be a better place.
   B. believers can know and be like Christ.
   C. you don't have to feel guilty.
   D. people treat you better.

10. **What should we do until Christ returns and we experience ultimate victory over the flesh?**
   A. Die to self
   B. Ignore the flesh
   C. Find life in Christ
   D. Both A and C

EXAM 12

What Do You Say?

Galatians 5:1 says, "It was for freedom that Christ set us free." Are you walking in the freedom of Christ?

Not completely.

Endnotes

Lesson 3 – Dying to Self

[1] Oswald Chambers, *My Utmost for His Highest* (Grand Rapids, MI: Discovery House, 1995), May 16.

Lesson 5 – Suffering

[1] Webster's Dictionary.

[2] Third verse of "How Firm a Foundation" by John Rippon, music by Joseph Funk.

Lesson 6 – Humility

[1] Parable told in Luke 14:7-14.

[2] Job's last defense can be read in Job chapters 29-32.

[3] Raphael Cardinal Merry del Val, *A Litany of Humility* (Chicago: Loyola University Press, 1963).

Lesson 8 – Walking in Truth, Part 1

[1] James Strong, *Strong's Exhaustive Concordance* (Peabody, MA: Hendrickson, 2007).

[2] The definitions of the Greek words were compiled from biblehub.com

Lesson 9 – Walking in Love

[1] Carmichael, *IF,* 10, 28, 30, 31, 33-36, 40, 43.

I have been crucified with Christ. It is no longer I who live, but Christ who lives in me. And the life I now live in the flesh I live by faith in the Son of God, who loved me and gave Himself for me.

—Galatians 2:20